PHOTOGRAPHY AND THE LAW

PHOTOGRAPHY AND THE LAW

Copyright • Obscenity • Liability
Invasion of Privacy

Christopher Du Vernet, M.A., LL.B

Self-Counsel Press
(a division of)
International Self-Counsel Press Ltd.
Canada U.S.A.

Printed in Canada

First edition: February, 1986
Second edition: August, 1991

Canadian Cataloguing in Publication Data

Du Vernet, Christopher.
  Photography and the law

  (Self-counsel legal series)
  ISBN 0-88908-666-4

  1. Photography — Law and legislation — Canada.
  2. Photography — Law and legislation — United States.
  I. Title. II. Series.
  KE2868.D82 1991   346.71'002'477   C91-091409-5
  KF3067.D82 1991

Cover photo by Images B.C., Vancouver

Self-Counsel Press
(*a division of*)
International Self-Counsel Press Ltd.
Head and Editorial Office
1481 Charlotte Road
North Vancouver, British Columbia V7J 1H1

U.S. Address
1704 N. State Street
Bellingham, Washington   98225

CONTENTS

SAMPLES

NOTICE TO READERS

Laws are constantly changing. Every effort is made to keep this publication as current as possible. However, neither the author nor the publisher can accept any responsibility for changes to the law or practice that occur after the printing of this publication. Please be sure that you have the most recent edition.

The reader is also reminded that while this book is the product of considerable research, it does not purport to be a conclusive survey of the law or a guide to every legal problem that may occur. Accordingly, if you are in doubt about a matter, or involved in any situation that may have legal consequences, a lawyer should be consulted.

ACKNOWLEDGMENTS

With few precedents in the field of photography and the law, this book has been a challenge to complete. Over 2,000 cases and hundreds of statutes were examined in the course of my research. Dozens of phone calls and interviews were made to ensure that the advice given here is not only legally accurate, but practical as well.

This work was undertaken with the support and assistance of several people, and I would like to express my gratitude to them. In particular, I would like to thank Mr. Hugh Segal, then President of Advance Planning & Communications Limited, and Senator Norman Atkins, then President of Camp Associates Advertising Limited for their encouragement and generous assistance in so many ways. As well, I would like to thank Blair McKenzie, General Counsel and Secretary of Torstar Corporation, who provided me with much of the legal training which made this book possible. Finally, I would like to thank my father and mother for their advice and support, and my wife Hellen, for her patience.

INTRODUCTION

In the United States alone, amateur photographers snap over 15 billion pictures a year, making photography one of the most popular recreational activities. Indeed, the versatility, portability, and affordability of the camera make photography a familiar part of North American life. Photography brings news and information to millions of readers and TV viewers. It is used to promote virtually every consumer product imaginable and photography is an important tool in judicial and scientific processes.

But because it is so easy, so simple, and so inexpensive to take a picture, photography is also a potential source of legal liability. Celebrities, entertainers, and other prominent people may not want their pictures taken. Governments may want to keep information secret. Professional photographers may not want others to use their work without permission. Accomplished athletes or artists may not want their pictures to be used in advertising. Art galleries or theaters may not want their shows photographed by patrons.

Just as millions of people go to great effort to take good photographs, millions of others go to equally great effort to prevent photographs being taken or used. The tension that exists between people who want to take photographs and those who do not want them taken, is at the heart of this book. Set out in the chapters which follow is a discussion of the law concerning photography in a variety of situations.

This book is not a conclusive statement on all areas of the law concerning photography, but you should find it very useful in determining *what* can be photographed, *how* a photograph can be taken, and *how* and *when* it can be used.

Chapter 1 discusses what the law permits and prohibits people from photographing. Chapter 2 discusses the important area of obscenity, including what the courts consider obscene and what uses may be made of obscene material. Chapter 3 discusses the manner in which a photograph should be taken and covers the law of negligence, trespassing, harassment, and the right to privacy. Chapter 4 discusses different ways a photograph may be used, such as in advertising, in the news, in judicial proceedings, and in photographic competitions. Chapter 5 discusses releases — what they are, when one should be obtained, and what form it should take. Chapter 6 discusses copyright, including its nature and benefits, how it is acquired, who owns it, how long it lasts, and how to prevent others from infringing on it. The final chapter looks at the business of photography — what to consider when getting insurance, negotiating contracts and credits, billing clients, and working with stock photo agencies.

This book includes both American and Canadian law, and will be useful not only for Americans and Canadians taking pictures in their own countries, but whenever they travel into the other country.

This comprehensive exploration of the law of photography will be an asset for every photographer, whether amateur or professional. Given the frequency with which a photographer could quite unwarily be confronted with legal issues, this book should be consulted frequently and should provide a helpful starting point for everyone who wishes his or her photography to be not only artistically accomplished, but useful and enduring as well.

1

WHAT CAN YOU PHOTOGRAPH?

One of your first considerations as a photographer is determining your subject matter. You must be sure that you have the right to photograph your subject. In Canada and the United States, there are definite limitations on your right to photograph currency, stamps, stocks and bonds, government information, buildings, judicial proceedings, people, and medical operations.

The rules and regulations for photographing these subjects differ depending on what jurisdiction you are working in. Generally speaking, because the United States permits individual states to regulate many areas which affect photographers, the laws in that country are more complicated and diverse.

These rules and regulations for photographing these subjects in both countries are specified in this chapter.

a. CURRENCY

1. United States

The United States restricts, but does not forbid, the photography of currency. The rules, however, are fairly complicated and a photographer should follow them closely to avoid difficulty.

As a general rule, making a photograph of the likeness of any currency of the United States, or of any foreign government, bank, or corporation, is a criminal offense under the United States Code.

However, there are several exceptions to the general rule. First, you can photograph currency for purposes of coin and stamp collecting, or to illustrate educational, historical, or news articles, or albums. But the photograph must be in black and white, and either less than three-quarters or more than one and one-half times the size of the currency it depicts.

Second, you can make or import motion picture films, microfilms, or slides of currency. However, no prints or other reproductions can be made from those films or slides without the permission of the Secretary of the Treasury, except for purposes of stamp and coin collecting, or to illustrate educational, historical, or news articles, books, journals, newspapers, or albums.

Third, although the photography of currency is prohibited for advertising purposes, legitimate coin and stamp dealers or publishers of articles, books, journals, newspapers, or albums on coins and stamps may publish photographs of paper money in philatetic or numismatic advertising. Still photographs used in such advertising can only depict paper money in black and white, and in a size less that three-fourths or more than one and one-half the money's actual size.

Finally, there are no restrictions on the photography of coins, except when this is done for the purposes of counterfeiting.

All the exceptions to the general rule concerning the photography of currency are found in section 474 of Title 18 of the United States Code. If you plan to take a picture of U.S. or foreign currency, you should follow the wording of that section carefully.

The penal laws of some states, such as New York, may prohibit or restrict the photography of instruments for the payment of money.

2. Canada

As a general rule, it is against the law in Canada to photograph the bank notes, paper money, or bank or government securities of any country. It is also against the law to print, make, distribute, or use any advertisement that shows the currency of any country. These acts are considered forms of counterfeiting, and are offenses under the Criminal Code. Persons convicted of counterfeiting are liable to imprisonment for up to five years.

However, there are two exceptions to this general rule. First, you are free to photograph currency that is no longer legal tender (that is, it could not be used today). Money issued by banks or governments that no longer exist, or that are no longer recognized can safely be photographed.

Second, photographing currency is not an offense if —

(a) there is no photography used at any stage in order to publish or print the likeness of the currency, except in connection with processes necessarily involved in transferring a finished drawing or sketch to a re-printed surface,

(b) except for the word "Canada," nothing has the appearance of a complete word, letter or numeral,

(c) no representation of a human face or figure is more than a general indication of features, without detail,

(d) no more than one color is used, and

(e) nothing in the likeness or appearance of the back of a current bank note or current paper money is published or printed in any form.

These provisions of the Criminal Code are intended to discourage any photography of currency.

This view was recently confirmed in a court decision in Ontario. In that case, an importer of novelties had been charged because he had imported ceramic mugs, ashtrays, ceramic savings banks, key chains, and playing cards that allegedly bore the likeness or appearance of the currency of Canada, the United States, and Italy.

The court interpreted the law broadly, and in its defense of doing so, quoted a letter written by the Deputy Governor of the Bank of Canada in 1954, when the issue was being debated. In his letter, the Deputy Governor stated:

> We have noted an increasing tendency for people to produce photographs and other reproductions of Bank of Canada notes, either for use in connection with commercial advertising or for some other purpose, or just as a matter of interest or curiosity. In such cases, the maker and users of the reproduction had no intention of passing off the pictures as currency or of making any wrongful use of the negatives or plates used in producing them. We believe, however, that it would be highly desirable if production of Canadian currency in this way could be prevented. For one thing, every such action tends to encourage others to imitate them or to think up new ways of making representations of currency, and generally cheapens the position of bank notes in the public eye. For another thing, once plates have been made, though for the most innocent purpose, they may pass into wrongful hands and be put to a wrongful purpose by persons who would not be able to produce the plates themselves.

The decision seems to shut the door on arguments that a photograph that isn't an exact likeness or appearance of currency should be acceptable. In the Ontario court's view, the similarity of the reproduction to the original item is not the issue; it is the impact on the esteem in which the currency is held and the possibility of the photographic negative eventually being put to a criminal use that is important.

b. STAMPS

1. United States

In the U.S., the photography of stamps is prohibited except for purposes of coin and stamp collecting, or to illustrate educational, historical, or news articles, books, journals, newspapers, or albums. Under the United States Code, the definition of postage stamps includes postage meter stamps.

As with currency, the Code prohibits photography of stamps for advertising purposes except by stamps dealers or publishers or articles, books, journals, newspapers, or albums on stamps for philatetic or numismatic advertising, under the following guidelines.

First, stamps may be photographed either in black and white or in color, and if the photograph is in color, and it depicts a *canceled* United States postage stamp, it may show the stamp in the exact size of a genuine stamp. On the other hand, if a color photograph depicts an *uncanceled* United States or foreign stamp, it must show the stamp either at less than three-quarters or more than one and one-half times the size of a genuine stamp.

If the photograph is in black and white, it may show a stamp in the exact size of a genuine stamp.

The law also permits photographers to make or import motion picture films, microfilms, or slides of postage and revenue stamps of the United States, and any foreign government, bank or corporation. No print or other reproduction can be made from such films except for purposes of coin and stamp collecting, or to illustrate educational, historical, or news articles, books, journals, newspapers, or albums, without the permission of the Secretary of the Treasury.

2. Canada

There appears to be no restriction on photographing a stamp in Canada unless it is done for counterfeiting or other fraudulent purposes. However, the retail marketing department of the Canada Post Corporation prefers photographers to request permission before any photographs are taken. They take the position that photography performed without permission is an offense under the Canada Post Corporation Act.

c. STOCKS AND BONDS

1. United States

As a general rule, it is unlawful to photograph a stock or bond of the United States of any foreign government, bank, or corporation.

However, photography of stocks and bonds is permitted for purposes of stamp and coin collecting, or to illustrate educational, historical, or news articles, books, journals, newspapers, or albums. As with currency, photographs made for such purposes must be in black and white, and depict the stock or bond in less than three-quarters or more than one and one-half times its actual size.

The photography of stocks and bonds for advertising purposes is prohibited, except for United States savings bonds, which may be reproduced to publicize a sale campaign.

Also, the penal laws of some states, such as New York, may prohibit or restrict the photography of stocks and bonds. You may want to ask an attorney if you are restricted in your state.

2. Canada

There is no general restriction on the photography of stocks and bonds in Canada, except when it is done for counterfeiting or other fraudulent purposes. The securities legislation of some provinces may, however, prohibit or limit such photography, and to be absolutely sure, photographers would be well advised to check all applicable legislation, regulations, rules, or guidelines issued by any provincial securities commission. Moreover, the issuer of a stock or bond may object to a photograph being taken on the basis of violation of copyright, passing off, or some other law.

In cases where the photograph is clearly not a duplicate of a stock or bond, however, it is unlikely that you would encounter legal difficulty. Also, a photograph made to promote the sale of the stock would likely be permissible regardless of copyright.

d. OFFICIAL SECRETS AND GOVERNMENT DOCUMENTS AND INFORMATION

1. United States

It is unlawful to take or sell a photograph of military and naval installations or equipment that have been defined by presidential order as requiring protection, without first having obtained permission to do so. Numerous installations and equipment have been so defined including —

(a) installations, publications, and equipment, classified as "top secret," "secret," "confidential," or "restricted," and,

(b) commercial establishments engaged in the development or manufacturing of classified arms or equipment.

If signs with these designations are posted on or outside installations or equipment, it is a criminal offense to photograph them without permission.

Further, it is illegal to disclose by any means (for example, by a photograph) to any unauthorized person, or use in a way that might harm the safety or interest of the country, information that has been designed as "classified." It has been ruled, however, that this regulation does not apply to historical documents.

2. Canada

Canada has one of the most sweeping acts governing official secrets of any western country. By virtue of the Official Secrets Act, it is illegal to photograph a broad range of locations and documents.

Locations that cannot be photographed are termed "prohibited places," and are defined in the act as follows:

a. any work of defense belonging to or occupied or used by or by or on behalf of Her Majesty including arsenals, armed forces establishments or stations, factories, dockyards, mines, mine fields, camps, ships, aircraft, telegraph, telephone, wireless or signal stations or offices, and places used for the purpose of building, repairing, making or storing any munitions of war or any sketches, plans, models or documents relating thereto, or for the purpose of getting any metal, oil or minerals of use in time of war;

b. any place not belonging to Her Majesty where any munitions of war or any sketches, models, plans or documents relating thereto, are being made, repaired, obtained, or stored under contract with, or with any person on behalf of, Her Majesty, or otherwise on behalf of Her Majesty; and

c. any place that is for the time being declared by order of the Governor in Council to be a prohibited place.

The government does not make a list of specific prohibited places available to the public.

Documents that cannot be photographed are those that concern a prohibited place, or contain information "that is calculated to be or might be or is intended to be directly or indirectly useful to a foreign power."

Where a photograph is taken of a prohibited place or document, the Official Secrets Act deems it to have been made for a purpose prejudicial to the safety or interests of the State unless the contrary is proved.

In one of the few other cases involving official secrets in Canada, it was held that the stamping of information as secret does not determine whether it is secret for the purposes of the Official Secrets Act; rather, it is the nature of the information itself and the circumstances surrounding it that determine the case. If the information has already been published or distributed publicly elsewhere, that would be relevant to a determination of its secrecy.

The vague wording of the act makes it difficult to know what can be photographed and what cannot. Accordingly, it is wise to avoid taking pictures of, or even having a camera, in the neighborhood of a military site. Equal care should be exercised with government documents which, unless commonly made available to the public, may be official secrets.

You should be aware that if you photograph a document, plan, model, sketch, or other piece of information that is not considered an official document, you may still be liable under other laws. You must be sure that the document is not covered by copyright, for example. (See chapter 6 for more on copyright.) Or, if you take the item to be photographed from someone's files, or you have someone take it for you (for example, your source) you run the risk of being charged with possession of stolen goods.

e. BUILDINGS

1. United States

(a) Inside

Anyone who has been to Washington, D.C. has probably marveled at the architecture of its public buildings. Owing to the number, prominence, and historical significance of public buildings in that city and in the rest of the country, Congress has enacted the following regulations governing photography of them.

These regulations, which apply to virtually every piece of federal property, provide that photographs may be taken in buildings occupied by a public agency only with the consent of the agency occupying that space, or a federal court order. Except where security regulations apply, or rule prohibits, photographs for news purposes may be taken at entrances, lobbies, foyers, corridors, or auditoriums, when used for public meetings. Subject to the foregoing prohibitions, photographs for advertising and commercial purposes may be taken only with the written permission of an authorized official of the public agency occupying the space. If you violate these regulations you may be fined not more than $50 or imprisoned for not more that 30 days, or both.

In addition to these general rules, specific rules have been enacted to govern photography in certain public buildings which are important to national security. For example, Pentagon building security regulations prohibit the presence or use of cameras except where they are carried and used by an official of the Department of Defense, the General Services administration, or press photographers who present proper passes. However, escorted tour visitors may carry cameras and take photographs only at designated points along a tour route.

In view of these regulations, it is wise to ask about photography before entering a public building. At most of the sites the average photographer would want to photograph pictures are permitted, and you will likely encounter problems only in the case of buildings that have some defense or security function.

The federal government is not the only building owner that controls or limits photography inside buildings. Often owners or operators of other buildings, such as theaters and museums, impose rules on patrons concerning photography of a performance or a display.

The right to impose such rules is derived from either the law of contract or the law of real property, depending on how the rule is imposed. In either case, if you do not observe the rule, the theater owner or operator generally reserves the right to eject you. They may also try to take your camera or film as well. This is completely illegal, and should be resisted. A court may decide that the photographs are the owner's property, and must be turned over to him or her. However, until the court decides otherwise, a theater patron is entitled to keep the film.

There are rules prohibiting photography in theaters for many reasons:

(a) The theater owner has a contract with a performer appearing at the theater requiring the owner to ensure that no photographs are taken of the performance without the performer's authorization. If a patron is then permitted to take photographs, the theater owner has violated the contract with the performer.

(b) Even without a contract, a photograph, especially when a flash is used, may disturb a performer. The performer may take action against the theater owner for failing to prevent such a disturbance.

(c) Even if there are no rules prohibiting photography in a theater, a performer may still be able to prevent photographs from being taken or, if they are taken, limit them to only personal use. The taking of photographs of an artistic performance may well violate the performer's copyright in his or her performance, where that performance is substantially reproduced. The performer could sue the photographer for copyright violation if photographs were taken without the performer's permission.

(d) Finally, some owners or operators of entertainment sites may prohibit photography on their property for other commercial reasons. For example, amusement parks may allow only certain parties the exclusive right to take and sell photographs of buildings, structures, or objects situated within their grounds. If the site operators then allowed the public to take photographs, they would be violating the exclusive agreement, and might be sued by those parties.

An exclusive arrangement like this was made by the operators of the New York World's Fair in 1964–1965. There, the corporation operating the fair reached agreement with another party to take and sell postcard pictures of the fair, its buildings, and objects in return for a royalty. However, another party, who had unsuccessfully submitted a bid for this exclusive right, took and sold postcard photographs without permission. The fair operators sought an injunction to prevent this other party from manufacturing postcards, albums, and other items that contained photographs taken at the fair. In granting the injunction, the court ruled that the World's Fair Grounds contained unique buildings, structures, and objects, and because the fair operators charged an admission fee, they had a property right. Accordingly, no party could photograph the fair's buildings, structures, or objects without permission.

(b) Outside

As a practical matter, virtually anyone is free to photograph the exterior of a building in the U.S. It is impossible to police such photography and to enforce any legal rights to prevent such photography unless some wide-scale reproduction of the photographs is made.

However, as a legal matter, there are some rules governing the photography of the exterior of buildings. If you are planning to photograph a building and make any commercial use of the photographs, it would be prudent to be aware of these rules.

In the U.S., copyright laws give protection to pictorial, graphic, and sculptural works. Such works are defined to include works of artistic craftsmanship insofar as their form, but not their mechanical or utilitarian aspects, is concerned. The design of a useful article (which is defined as an article having an intrinsic utilitarian function) is considered a pictorial, graphic, or sculptural work only to the extent that such design incorporates pictorial, graphic, or sculptural features that can be identified separately from, and are capable of existing independently of, the utilitarian aspects of the article.

This means that the exterior of a building may be photographed unless the building displays some pictorial, graphic, or sculptural features apart from the utilitarian aspects of its structure. For example, sculptures of griffins, gremlins, or other mythological figures which are often placed on the corners and other prominent points of old buildings, are sculptural features separate from a building's design. For this reason, they may be protected by copyright, and therefore cannot be photographed.

The question remains as to whether a building can be considered part of a performance or show in which an owner can have a legally recognized property right. The effect of the New York World Fair's case, mentioned above, may be that a unique building, structure, or object is a show, much like a theatrical or musical performance, and so no one may photograph it without permission of the owner. This would result in tremendous commercial difficulties. However, it's unlikely that this case will be interpreted in this way, since the operators of the World's Fair charged admission and, therefore, had a property right in any photographs.

The owner or operator of a building to which the public has unrestricted access has no right to protect and can be considered to have waived any rights. However, how this whole issue is resolved remains to be seen.

Section 105 of the U.S. Copyright Act provides that copyright protection is not available for any work of the U.S. Government, so any problems that may arise as a result of the New York World's Fair case will probably not apply to public buildings. If copyright protection is extended to include the exterior of a building, it will not include the exterior of a building owned by the government. People are apparently free to photograph, and to reproduce photographs, of such buildings.

2. Canada

(a) Inside

The owners of many buildings, both public and private, prohibit the public from taking photographs inside them. A photographer who violates these prohibitions may be acting unlawfully and can, depending on the circumstances, face a civil or a criminal action.

Theaters, art galleries, and museums are the buildings in which photography is most likely to be prohibited. Often in theaters there is a term in the contract between the entertainer and the theater that the theater will prevent patrons from taking pictures of the entertainer's performance. If patrons do take photographs, then the theater is in breach of its contract and may be sued for damages by the performer. Accordingly, theaters frequently make it a condition of entrance that the patrons not take pictures. Anyone who does so may be ejected by the theater and sued by it.

If the theater and performer did not have such a contract, the performer, depending on the nature of the performance and the extent of the photographic record made of it, could still sue if a patron took pictures of this performance. In such a case, the performer would base the action on the Copyright Act, which makes it unlawful to produce or reproduce a work or any part of it in any form without permission of the copyright owner.

Art galleries and museums also often have a term in the contract between the institution and a party who has lent a work or a display to it that the gallery or museum will prevent visitors from taking pictures of the items exhibited. If visitors do take photographs, then the gallery or museum is in breach of contract and may be sued for damages by the owner of the item. Accordingly, galleries and museums also make it a condition of entrance that visitors not take pictures. Anyone who does so may, just as in the case of a theater patron, be ejected and sued.

14

Even galleries and museums which do not have such contractual obligations, frequently prohibit visitors from taking pictures of works on display. Such prohibitions are most likely to be instituted because the gallery or museum wishes to protect their own copyright in the work. As discussed below, it is a violation of copyright to photograph a painting or sculpture situated in a private place or building without the owner's permission.

Many public buildings, such as the Ontario Legislature and the House of Commons in Ottawa, prohibit the taking of photographs in certain areas, such as in rooms where public representatives are meeting. Such prohibitions are enacted for security reasons. If you disobey these rules, you will, no doubt, be asked to leave, but it is not likely that you'll be charged with an offense.

If you are ejected from a public or private building for taking unauthorized photographs, the owners of the building are not entitled to take your camera or film. The camera and film are your property, and remain so until a court orders otherwise. However, Section 38 of the Copyright Act provides that all infringing copies of any work in which copyright subsists, and all plates used or intended to be used for the production of such infringing copies, are the property of the copyright owner, who may sue in order to gain possession or compensation. The owner of a theater, art gallery, or museum, or of work appearing or being performed there, could be entitled to any film taken by a photographer without permission. However, this would only be so after a court decided that the photography had occurred wrongfully and ordered the film to be delivered up to the building owner.

(b) Outside

Anyone may photograph the outside of any building in Canada. Section 27(2)(c) of the Copyright Act provides that anyone may take and publish a photograph of an architectural work of art, such as the outside of a building, or a painting, drawing, engraving, or work of sculpture or artistic craftsmanship that is permanently situated in a public place or building.

f. JUDICIAL PROCEEDINGS

1. United States

The Supreme Court of each state is responsible for instituting rules concerning the photography of judicial proceedings. These rules are called "canons of judicial conduct" and bind all courts in that state.

In devising these rules, state courts have frequently followed the canons of judicial conduct developed by the American Bar Association (ABA). The current ABA canon concerning photography is Canon 3, which provides that "a judge should maintain order and decorum in the courtroom." Essentially, the canon calls upon the highest court of each state to prohibit photography unless rules are developed that ensure it will be unobtrusive and not interfere with the right of the parties to a fair trial. This recommendation has given state authorities a great deal of latitude, and has resulted in a variety of approaches to photography in court.

Many states provide that individual trial participants can, in effect, veto coverage of their own courtroom appearances. In some states, all trial participants must agree to camera coverage; in others, any individual participant can order cameras to be removed from the portion of the trial in which he or she participates.

Two states have gone further in allowing photography in the courtroom. Both Florida and Wisconsin have rules that make courtroom photography dependent only on the decision of the judge, not on the decision of any participant. Participants may request photographers to be excluded, but they must give the court a convincing reason why their request should be granted.

In Florida, guidelines have been instituted so that no more than one television camera and one camera technician are allowed. Existing recording systems must be used and where more than one broadcast news organization wants to cover a trial, the media must pool coverage. No artificial lighting is allowed; equipment must be positioned in a fixed location and may not be moved during the trial; film, video-tape, and lenses may not be changed while the court is in session; the jury must not be filmed; and the judge may, at his or her discretion, exclude coverage of certain witnesses.

The Florida Supreme Court instituted this rule after a yearlong experiment with television. In announcing its new rule, the court stated that on balance there is more to be gained than lost by permitting electronic media coverage of judicial proceedings.

In Wisconsin, the rule is not as liberal as in Florida, in that courtroom photography is not allowed in certain types of cases. Ordinarily, however, photography is permitted unless a participant convinces the court it should not be allowed.

The constitutionality of Florida's rule was recently considered in the Supreme Court, and fortunately for photographers, was upheld. The issue arose after two Miami Beach police officers were convicted by a Florida trial court of conspiring to commit burglary, grand larceny, possession of burglary tools, and breaking and entering into a well-known Miami Beach restaurant. In keeping with Florida's policy, a TV camera was allowed to film the trial, which was ultimately broadcast on Florida television.

Following their conviction, the accused moved for a new trial, arguing that because of the TV coverage, they had been denied a fair hearing. The Supreme Court rejected their appeal, concluding that a state could legitimately provide for radio, TV, and still photography coverage of a criminal trial for public broadcast, notwithstanding the objection of the defendants.

Having survived this court challenge, the Florida rule may provide to be the wave of the future for courtroom photography. Whether more states will follow Florida's lead is hard to tell. But, at the time of writing, at least 17 states were experimenting, or had just concluded experimentation, with courtroom photography.

Whatever a state's rules on courtroom photography happen to be, violation of them can amount to criminal contempt. Texas TV news photographer William Seymour found this out the hard way.

On March 11, 1966, he took TV photographs of a defendant and his attorney in the hallway outside a courtroom as the defendant was being led from the courtroom at the end of the proceedings. The Texas rules at the time prohibited the "taking of photographs or broadcasting or televising in connection with any judicial proceedings on or from the same floor of the building in which courtrooms are located." Seymour was spotted and cited for contempt for having violated this rule. In due course, he was convicted.

But there is still hope for photographers in states with rules restricting courtroom photography. In some circumstances, these rules can be interpreted in a photographer's favor.

A good illustration is a case involving the Oklahoma Publishing Company. The case concerned a state statute providing that juvenile hearings were closed unless specifically opened to the public by court order. A railroad switchman had been shot to death, and on July 29, 1976, an 11-year-old boy, Larry Donald Brewer, appeared at a detention hearing in Oklahoma County Juvenile Court on charges alleging second degree murder in the shooting of the switchman. According to the judgment given on appeal in the case, reporters, including one from the Oklahoma Publishing Company, were present in the courtroom during the hearing and learned the juvenile's name. As the boy was escorted from the courthouse to a vehicle, one of the Oklahoma Publishing Company's photographers took his picture. Later, a number of stories using the boy's name and photograph were printed in newspapers in the county, including three newspapers owned by the Oklahoma Publishing Company. As well, radio stations broadcast the boy's name and television stations showed film footage and identified him by name.

The District Court of Oklahoma City, in keeping with the State's statute concerning juvenile hearings, made a pre-trial ruling prohibiting members of the news media from publishing the boy's name and picture.

The Oklahoma Publishing Company challenged the order on the basis that the first and fourteenth amendments of the U.S. Constitution would not permit a state court to prohibit publication of widely disseminated information obtained at court proceedings which had, in fact, been open to the public earlier.

The court upheld the company's petition. It declared that because the press had been present with full knowledge of all of the parties and had acquired its information lawfully, the name and picture of the juvenile were in the public domain, and the order prohibiting their publication violated the first and fourteenth amendments.

2. Canada

(a) Restrictions

Generally, you cannot take pictures in or around a courtroom in Canada. The law may also prohibit the publication of photographs of people involved in, or evidence relating to, certain types of trials.

These rules are based on a judge's historical power to control people's behavior in and around the courtroom and to ensure that the administration of justice is not brought into disrepute. This power is codified in the Criminal Code and in the rules of practice of various provinces.

An example of the exercise of this power occurred in 1976 in Peel County, Ontario, when a cameraman covering a criminal trial persisted in taking pictures of the participants and the judge. Believing that the cameraman's behavior would intimidate those involved and adversely affect the atmosphere in which the trial was conducted, the judge made an order forbidding photography of participants not only inside, but outside the courthouse as well.

(b) The Young Offenders Act

One of the most important considerations of photographing judicial proceedings in Canada is the Young Offenders Act. This act has attracted extensive criticism for its restrictions on the dissemination of information of trials. The act governs the trials of young people, who are defined as being those between 12 and 18 years of age.

The act essentially prohibits anyone from publishing by any means a report that identifies a young person who is involved in legal proceedings. The young person could be an offender, an alleged offender, a witness, or a victim. Therefore, a photograph would almost certainly be covered. However, a court may lift the protection of the law.

Further, if a young person is transferred to an adult court, and either the young person or the prosecutor requests, the judge must take an order directing that any information about the offense presented at the transfer hearing may be published in any newspaper before the trial is ended. ("Newspaper" is defined in the act as including any paper, magazine, or periodical published more frequently than once a month.)

Because of the restrictive nature of the Young Offenders Act, a photographer should not publish a picture of a young person involved in a judicial proceeding.

(c) Controversial matters

Canadian law also prohibits the publication of photographs of people involved in, or of evidence relating to trials dealing with certain controversial matters. For example, if an accused person is charged with incest, gross indecency, sexual assault, sexual assault with a weapon, threats to a third party, causing bodily harm, or aggravated sexual assault, either the accused or the prosecutor can request an order directing that the identity of the complainant, and any information shall not be published in any newspaper or broadcast. The judge, on his or her own initiative, may also make such as order.

Where an order has been made, no photograph of the complainant should be published or broadcast. These rules also apply to preliminary hearings.

Photographers should also be aware that it is an offense to print or publish —

in relation to any judicial proceedings any indecent matter or indecent medical, surgical or physiological details, being matter or details that, if published, are calculated to injure public morals. (Section 166, Criminal Code.)

Technical publications intended for circulation among members of the legal or medical profession are exempt from this rule.

It is very difficult to determine exactly what kind of matter is "calculated to injure public morals." There is little, if any, judicial guidance on the interpretation of this phrase, and photographers should exercise caution when covering trails.

(d) Bail hearings

Bail hearings are another judicial proceedings where photographers should be careful. A judge must make an order prohibiting publication of any evidence or information given at the bail hearing if the accused requests. The prosecutor may also make such a request, but the judge is not obliged to grant it.

While this area of the law does not refer specifically to photography, there may be circumstances where publication of a photograph of the accused, or some evidence relating to the crime, may violate an order.

g. PEOPLE

If you want to photograph your next-door neighbor as she suntans in her backyard, can you? Are you free to photograph people as they walk down the street whether they want their picture taken or not? If you want to photograph a singer as he performs on stage, do you have legal grounds to do so?

When you photograph people, you face two issues. First, you must determine whether or not you can take someone's picture in a particular situation at all. Second, you must know what you can and cannot do with the person's picture once you have taken it. This section explains when you can and cannot take someone's picture; chapter 4 details how you may use a photograph.

1. United States

Lawsuits are one of the many means people use to hinder or prevent photographers from taking their picture. While lawsuits are unpleasant for the parties involved, they are generally good news for photographers, for as a result of legal actions, a substantial body of case law and legislation dealing with photographers' rights and obligations has been created.

The law varies from state to state. Some states give considerably less recognition than others to the right of people to lead lives out of the public eye. One reason for different approaches to privacy statutes is because there are different levels of entertainment and communications activity in different states. For example, most movies are made in California and most magazines are headquartered in New York. Because of the concentration of media and entertainment people in those two states, the question of photographing people has arisen frequently. New York and California have well developed laws; indeed, New York could well be regarded as the pioneer in this area, as it passed the first right to privacy statute in the U.S.

In states with privacy statutes, certain general principles or guidelines have developed for photographing people. First, there are no restrictions on a photographer's general freedom to take pictures of people. Accordingly, unless such photography involves the violation of some other rule of law, such as the law of trespass or harassment, a photographer is free to photograph another person, whether or not that person consents.

Despite the laissez-faire approach, courts in states with right to privacy statutes will nevertheless intervene when a person has been photographed in circumstances that are shocking to the reasonable person. For example, courts have awarded damages against news photographers who without consent have photographed hospital patients as they lay in their beds.

While the manner in which a photograph is taken of a person may not be objectionable, its use may be. In other words, just because you take someone's photograph does not mean you may use that photograph for any purpose. The right to privacy statutes of most states specifically prohibit a person from using another's photograph in advertising or for purposes of trade without that other person's consent. (For more detail on taking and using photographs in states with privacy laws, see chapters 3 and 4.)

In those states without right to privacy statutes, guidelines for photographing people depend on whether or not the state's courts have recognized a right to privacy. If they have, the rules are generally similar to those set out above. If they have not, photographers are generally free to photograph other people no matter how distasteful or upsetting such photography may be.

An extreme example of the liberty accorded photographers in states that do not recognize the right of privacy is a 1956 Wisconsin case in which a court dismissed a complaint brought by a woman who alleged that the defendant, a tavern keeper, had entered the ladies' restroom of the tavern to take a picture of her.

Other laws exist that govern whether or not a photographer may take another person's picture. Such laws generally exist independent of any right to privacy a state may recognize.

For example, you may be prevented from taking pictures of people in an accident if the police believe that your presence interferes with their work. As well, trespass laws may make it illegal to photograph another person if you go onto that person's land or premises without permission.

As well, the law with respect to harassment may make it illegal for a photographer to take another's picture in certain circumstances. An excellent illustration of the application of harassment law is the case of *Galella vs. Onassis*, where the widow of a former President successfully sued a photographer for invasion of her privacy, assault, and several other torts, where he persistently followed her, bumped into her, and disturbed her and her children in an attempt to photograph the family.

Moreover, it may be against the law to take a person's picture in a certain place. For example, it may be an offense to take pictures of participants in a court proceeding in or around the place where a trial is held. In certain states such photography is prohibited in the interest of conducting a fair trial.

Finally, it may be a breach of contract or license for a photographer to take a picture of someone in certain circumstances. Where someone attends a theatrical or musical performance, it may be a term of that person's contract or license with the theater owner that no one will take pictures of the performance. Such terms are perfectly legal and enforceable where they can genuinely be considered to have been part of the parties' agreement. To be part of the agreement, the term must reasonably be brought to a theater patron's attention before, or at the time of, the purchase of a ticket.

2. Canada

Generally, you cannot go onto another person's property to take his or her picture. You cannot persistently follow a person from place to place in an attempt to photograph him or her, and you cannot continually watch a person's house or place of business in the hope of getting a photograph. Also, you have no right to impede, molest, or obstruct a person in an attempt to take a picture. Short of these prohibitions, however, you are basically free to take another person's picture, and legally there is nothing the other person can do about it.

You may, for example, take a person's picture as he or she walks down the street. You may photograph your neighbor from your own property, whether your neighbor is outside or can be seen through a window, and you can fly over someone's house and take a picture as long as your flight path does not violate air traffic regulations.

Canadian law has never allowed a person to prevent another person from taking the first person's picture, except in circumstances where some other legal right, such as the right to sue and enjoy property, or the right to go about business without interference, has been violated. Canadian courts have traditionally considered the risk of being photographed while in public view as something inherent in civilized life. (See the section on right to privacy in chapter 3 for more details.)

h. MEDICAL CASES

1. United States

It is well established law in the United States that a hospital patient may not be photographed without the patient's consent, either by a doctor or by anyone else for purposes other than treatment.

The leading case on this issue concerned Henry Berthiaume, who was suffering from cancer of the larynx. His doctor decided to take a picture of him while he was in hospital. On what turned out to be the last day of Berthiaume's life, the doctor raised the dying man's head, placed some blue operating room towelling under it, and then took several photographs. During this activity, Berthiaume appeared to protest by raising a clenched fist and moving his head in an attempt to get out of the camera's range. Berthiaume's wife also told the doctor that she did not think that her husband wanted his picture taken.

After Berthiaume's death, his wife sued the doctor for invasion of privacy, and for assault and battery of her husband. In a strongly worded decision, the court rejected the doctor's argument that he was entitled to take photographs of his patients without consent as part of his medical records.

The court stated that —

> an individual has the right to decide whether that which is his shall be given to the public, and not only to restrict and limit but also to withhold absolutely his talents, property, or other subjects of the right of privacy from all dissemination. The facial characteristics or peculiar cast of one's features, whether normal or distorted, belong to the individual, and may not be reproduced without his permission. Even a photographer who is authorized to take a portrait is not justified in making or retaining additional copies for himself.

As this case suggests, American courts will have no hesitation awarding damages against a photographer who takes a picture of a hospital patient without the patient's consent.

As a Missouri court noted in a case where a photographer from a news picture syndicate surreptitiously photographed a patient hospitalized because of her insatiable appetite, any right of privacy ought to protect a person from publication of a picture taken without consent while ill or in bed for treatment and recuperation.

2. Canada

To most North Americans, the movie *The Elephant Man* was merely a touching story about a Victorian man, John Merrick, who suffered from a disease which grossly distorted the shape of his head and body. As far as they knew, the disease had become as dead as its most famous sufferer.

But one day in the summer of 1985, residents of Toronto discovered that this disease is still with us. On August 21, 1985, the *Toronto Star* published photographs of a 13-year-old Guyanese boy, Gary Rangasamy, who was a patient in Scarborough General Hospital suffering from "Elephant Man's disease." Apparently the boy and his family gave the *Star* permission to take and publish numerous photographs of the boy's misshapen hand and arm. The pictures showed the boy's limb grown to three times its normal size, flabby, and useless.

The photography of Gary Rangasamy, and of other hospital patients and medical operations is of considerable public interest. With so many new types of medical procedures — organ transplants, treatment for AIDS, and the birth of test tube babies — photographers and patients are increasingly concerned about their rights.

Canadian law is surprisingly silent on this issue. The sole legal authority that might apply is legislation requiring medical personnel to keep medical records confidential.

Despite the lack of Canadian law, certain basic legal principles exist that would probably favor a patient's privacy if a case were to go to court. A patient could probably successfully argue at least one of the following:

(a) His or her privacy had been violated by the photographer and the hospital

(b) The medical facility violated a term of an implied contract for services that it would not permit dignity or privacy to be disturbed

(c) The photographer and any medical personnel who assisted the photographer committed a battery if the patient was touched

Most of Canada's foremost hospitals take steps to prevent photographers from entering patients' rooms or having access to their records without permission. Some hospitals, however, do not feel that a patient's right to privacy is absolute and do permit photographers to take pictures in some circumstances. Specifically, if a patient has an affliction that would interest medical students, hospitals will sometimes photograph a patient and use the picture for teaching purposes.

Despite the benefits to science that may accrue from such practices, it is my belief that such photography, unless expressly consented to by the patient, is a serious violation of the patient's legal rights and could be the basis of a successful court action by the patient against the hospital and all medical personnel involved. A patient comes to a hospital to be treated, not to be made a spectacle. A patient consents to be treated, but agrees to nothing more. In my view, a Canadian court would likely award significant damages against those who failed to observe this principle.

2
WHAT MAKES A PHOTOGRAPH OBSCENE?

The wide-scale acceptance of sexually explicit materials poses a challenge to those charged with the task of enforcing obscenity laws. The courts have struggled for years to define obscenity, and in the opinion of many, they still have not succeeded.

a. WHAT IS OBSCENE IN THE UNITED STATES?

American courts have struggled for well over a century to define obscenity, and, in the opinion of at least one U.S. Supreme Court Justice, they still have not succeeded.

Not everyone shares this pessimistic assessment, but all would agree that current definitions are vague, imprecise, and unpredictable in their application.

This uncertainty is a source of great concern for photographers, for many of whom the nude is a legitimate and frequently used subject. While it has been held that nudity is not necessarily obscene, the hundreds of decisions given by state and federal courts on this question indicate that the nude is not necessarily acceptable either. Where the dividing line will be drawn in any given case, no one can tell.

The current legal definition of obscenity is derived partly from regulations implemented by individual states and partly from standards for the entire country developed by the U.S. Supreme Court. It is impossible to canvass all the varied state regulations here, so the discussion below shall focus solely on federal law and standards.

On June 21, 1973, the Supreme Court handed down five major obscenity decisions. These decisions, which guide both state and federal courts to this day, were significant because they laid down new, more restrictive guidelines for determining obscenity.

Of the five, the most important is the case of *Miller vs. California*. Miller had conducted a mass mailing of advertising brochures promoting the sale of four pornographic books. These brochures consisted primarily of pictures and drawings that, in the court's words, "very explicitly" depicted men and women in groups of two or more engaging in a variety of sexual activities.

One of Miller's brochures was received by the manager of a restaurant in Newport Beach, California, and his mother. They complained to the police, and Miller was charged with violation of the California Penal Code, which made it an offense to knowingly distribute obscene material. Miller was convicted, and he appealed to the Supreme Court.

In this case decision, the first since 1957 in which a majority of the Supreme Court was able to agree on a test for obscenity, the court set out several principles by which obscene material should be identified. In an historic decision, the court confirmed that the states have legitimate interest in prohibiting the dissemination or exhibition of obscene material and such material is not protected by the first amendment.

In determining what should be considered obscene, the Supreme Court decided that state courts should follow three basic guidelines. They are as follows:

(a) Whether "the average person, applying contemporary community standards" would find the work, taken as a whole, appeals to the prurient interest

(b) Whether the work depicts or describes, in a patently offensive way, sexual conducts specifically defined by the applicable state law

(c) Whether the work taken as a whole lacks serious literary, artistic, political, or scientific value

The Supreme Court did not suggest how the state governments should regulate these guidelines, but it did give a few examples of what a state statute could define for regulation under the second guideline:

(a) Patently offensive representations or descriptions of ultimate sexual acts, normal or perverted, actual or simulated

(b) Patently offensive representations or descriptions of masturbation, excretory functions, and lewd exhibition of the genitals

The Supreme Court labelled this kind of material as "hard core."

In making community standards the tool for determining what state courts should find obscene, the court stressed that the community to which it was referring was something less than a national one. Calling attempts to define a national community standard "an exercise in futility," the court stated, "our nation is simply too big and too diverse for this Capital Court to reasonably expect that such standards could be articulated for all 50 states in a single formulation, even assuming the prerequisite consensus exists."

Despite the confidence with which the Supreme Court announced this decision, it is still hard to know what photography will be considered obscene. It is probably accurate to say that the vast majority of photographic studies of nudes will not be considered obscene under the Supreme Court's guidelines. Indeed, it has been the law for many years that nudity is not generally obscene. However, in cases where the artistic elements are displaced by other aspects, the court's reaction will be more difficult to predict.

The result of the "local community" requirement, for example, has already resulted in widely varying responses to the same material. A photographer whose work has survived judicial scrutiny in one state cannot know with reasonable certainty whether he or she can safely distribute it across the country.

This problem is not helped by the qualification imposed by the Supreme Court that local community standards must be those of an average person. In a decision given one year after the Miller case, the Supreme Court held that it is sufficient if the allegedly obscene material is shown to the court, and the jury (or, in the absence of a jury, the judge) decides according to its own opinion of the average person's tolerances. This decision confirmed the holdings of numerous state courts that consistently maintained that pornographic material "speaks for itself."

b. PROHIBITED USES OF OBSCENITY IN THE UNITED STATES

Both state and federal law regulate the use of obscene materials; federal law only will be discussed in this section.

Obscenity at the federal level is governed mainly by sections of the United States Code. These sections deal with mail, transportation, and the importance of obscene matter.

1. Mail

The U.S. postal service will not deliver envelopes, wrappers, and postal cards that have on them any "delineations...of an indecent, lewd, lascivious or obscene character." This includes photographs. Anyone who knowingly deposits such material for mailing or delivery, or knowingly takes it from the mails for the purpose of circulating or disposing of it, is guilty of an offense.

A person who mails obscene materials can be found guilty even if he or she doesn't know that the materials are obscene; it is sufficient that the prosecution show that the person knows the contents, character, and nature of the materials. However, the person who *receives* the obscene material, and intends it for personal use, is not liable.

The United States Code permits the postal service to dispose of materials that are "non-mailable" or obscene. Usually, the material is destroyed.

Finally, the United States Code sets out certain prohibitions for mailing sexually oriented advertisements. A sexually oriented advertisement is "any advertisement that depicts, in actual or simulated form, or explicitly describes, in a predominantly sexual context, human genitalia, any act of natural or unnatural sexual intercourse, any act of sadism or masochism, or any other erotic subject directly related to the foregoing."

Anyone who mails sexually oriented advertisements must place on the envelope or cover his or her name and address and a notice as required by the postal service. Any person may then request the post office to eliminate such material from his or her mail delivery. The postal service keeps a list of people who make these requests and no one may mail any sexually oriented advertisement to any individual whose name and address has been on the list for more than 90 days. The post office will get a court order prohibiting anyone who mails a sexually-oriented advertisement to a person on their list from continuing to do so.

2. Transportation

An important provision for every photographer is paragraph 1465 of Title 18 of the United States Code.

This section covers the transportation of obscene matters for sale or distribution. It reads as follows:

> Whoever knowingly transports in interstate or foreign commerce for the purpose of sale or distribution any obscene, lewd, lascivious, or filthy book, pamphlet, picture, film paper...print, silhouette,...figure, image...or any other matter

of indecent or immoral character, shall be fined not more than $5,000 or imprisoned not more than 5 years, or both.

The transportation as aforesaid of two or more copies of any publication or two or more of any article of the character described above, or a combined total of five such publications and articles, shall create a presumption that such publications or articles are intended for sale or distribution, but such presumptions shall be rebuttable.

When any person is convicted of a violation of this act, the Court in its judgment of conviction may, in addition to the penalty prescribed, order the confiscation and disposal of such items described herein which were found in the possession or under the immediate control of such person at the time of his arrest.

A similar prohibition is in paragraph 1462 of Title 18 of the United States Code concerning the importation and transportation of obscene matters. It reads as follows:

Whoever brings into the United States, or any place subject to the jurisdiction thereof, or knowingly uses any express company or other common carrier, for carriage in interstate or foreign commerce —

> a. any obscene, lewd, lascivious, or filthy book, pamphlet, picture, motion picture, film, paper, … or other matter of indecent character; or…
>
> c. … any … article, or thing designed, adapted, or intended for…any indecent or immoral use; or any written or printed card, letter, circular, book, pamphlet, advertisement, or notice of any kind giving information directly or indirectly where, or of whom, or by what means any of such mentioned articles, matters, or things may be obtained or made; or

Whoever knowingly takes from such express company or other common carrier any matter or thing the carriage of which is herein made unlawful—shall be fined not more than $ 5,000 or imprisoned not more than 5 years, or both …

The Supreme Court has affirmed on several occasions that this section may constitutionally apply to shipments of matter to an adult for his or her private use. The most recent of these decisions is *U.S. vs. Orito*, one of the four decisions rendered with the Miller case. In that decision, the U.S. Supreme Court held that given:

(a) that the obscene material is not protected under the first amendment, and

(b) that the government has a legitimate interest in protecting the public commercial environment by preventing obscene material from entering the stream of commerce, and

(c) that no constitutionally protected privacy is involved, the constitution permits comprehensive federal regulation of interstate transportation of obscene material, even though such transport may be private carriage, or material may be intended for the private use of the transporter.

It has also been held that both the sender and the recipient of obscene material can be held liable under this section.

3. Importation

A final provision important to photographers is paragraph 1305 of Title 19, which concerns the importation of obscene materials. That section prohibits all persons from

> importing into the United States from any foreign country ... any obscene book, pamphlet, paper, ... advertisement, circular, print, picture, ... or other representation ... or image on or of paper or other material...or other article which is obscene or immoral....

This paragraph permits customs officials to seize obscene materials and transmit them to a lawyer to start proceedings to forfeit and destroy the material. This type of material may be seized even if it is for the importer's private, personal use and possession and not for commercial purposes.

The paragraph contains an important exception for classical literature. It provides that —

> the Secretary of the Treasury may, in his discretion, admit the so-called classics or books of recognized and established literary or scientific merit, but may, in his discretion, admit such classics or books only when imported for non-commercial purposes.

Numerous court decisions have held that this exception is not the sole means by which scientists and scholars can import material for their study alone, which would be obscene in the hands of the general public.

For example, in a 1957 New York case, the special research department of a state university attempted to import photographs for use in the study of human sexual behavior. The material was seized by customs. When the university disputed the seizure, the court ruled in its favor on the basis that the photographs were not obscene because they wouldn't have sexual appeal to the people who would have access to them.

c. WHAT IS OBSCENE IN CANADA?

The latest attempt by the Supreme Court of Canada to interpret and enforce Canada's obscenity laws occurred in May, 1985. That judgment will undoubtedly form the basis of decisions in lower courts across Canada for some time to come. Therefore, photographers should be familiar with it. Be warned, though, that this decision may not give you any better idea of what actually constitutes obscenity; however, you will have a better understanding of the approach Canadian courts will take in the future.

The decision, involving Towne Cinema Theatres, reflects the difficulty that Canadian courts have had in dealing with obscenity. All of the justices participating in the decision agreed with the standard to be applied and the result of the application on the facts of the case, but they agreed for different reasons. Specifically, they disagreed on what the standard to be applied actually means, and what evidence should be used to prove whether it has been exceeded.

The case arose when the owner and manager of Towne Cinema Theatres was charged with presenting an obscene motion picture, *Dracula Sucks*. The charge was brought under section 163 of the Criminal Code, which defines obscene material as something that has as —

> a dominant characteristic ... the undue exploitation of sex, or of sex and any one or more of the following subjects, namely crime, horror, cruelty, and violence ...

At the trial, the defense submitted evidence showing that the film had been approved and classified by the censor boards of every province as a restricted adult movie, and that it had been previously been seen by several thousand people in Alberta.

The trial judge convicted the theater owner who subsequently appealed, arguing that the trial judge had not applied the proper test of obscenity. The Supreme Court thus had the task of determining what that test should be.

The justices considered the obscenity issue from the traditional point of view of "community standards." While all of the judges agreed that community standards was the test by which "undue exploitation" should be determined, they disagreed as to what was meant by such standards, and what evidence should be considered in determining whether the material being considered in a particular case exceeded them. The judges' opinions are important to understanding the final decision.

Three judges took the position that Canadian community standards means not what Canadians think is right for themselves to see, but what Canadians would not abide other Canadians seeing because it would go beyond our contemporary standard of tolerance. As well, in the opinion of the

37

three judges, the audience that would see the material was an important consideration, since the community may tolerate different things for different groups of people depending on the circumstances.

The three judges also took the position that while evidence of community standards of tolerance was useful, it was not essential. It is the opinion of the jury (or if there is no jury, the judge) that is important.

Three other judges took a different view. While agreeing that Canadian community standards means what Canadians would not abide other Canadians seeing, they felt that the audience to which the material was exposed was irrelevant. Two of these three judges also agreed with the first three that evidence of community standards of tolerance was not necessary. The third judge felt that the Crown should present some evidence.

The seventh judge phrased the Canadian community standards test yet another way. In her opinion, the *degree* of exploitation of sex that Canadians will accept is the important determining factor. She called this the Canadian standard of tolerance, or "tolerance in the sense of moral acceptability." The audience that sees the material is, in her view, irrelevant. She also felt that the Crown must present evidence on the issue of community standards.

The end result was that the appeal was granted and a new trial ordered.

It would seem from this case that a majority of the Supreme Court of Canada believes that evidence as to Canadian standards of tolerance, while useful, is not necessary. Beyond that, however, the judgment does not stand as a clear statement of a particular philosophy or approach. It remains unclear, for example, whether the community standard of tolerance means what Canadians would not abide other Canadians seeing, or whether it means the degree of exploitation of sex

Canadians at any given time will accept. This difference may be significant in future cases. As well, it is unclear what consideration, if any, should be given to the audience to which the material in question is to be exposed.

This uncertainty poses problems for photographers, as they can never be sure if a particular work will be acceptable or not until after a court has ruled on it. Moreover, they may have to bear the considerable expense and inconvenience of a trial to receive that determination.

Given such uncertainty, it would not be surprising if the Criminal Code's obscenity provisions were challenged as unconstitutional. And, indeed, such a challenge has been made. A Victoria, British Columbia video store, Red Hot Video Ltd., appealed a conviction to the Supreme Court for selling obscene materials. The basis of appeal was that the Criminal Code provisions were too vague, broad, and unreasonable to survive Canada's Charter of Rights and Freedoms, which guarantees fundamental justice as well as freedom of expression. The Supreme Court, however, refused to hear Red Hot Video's appeal. No reasons were given for this refusal.

Despite this uncertainty, there is some comfort in the Canadian law's approach to obscenity. First, the Supreme Court's decision in Towne Cinema Theatres reaffirms the application of a national standard. This may benefit photographers in smaller centers, where the local standard of tolerance may be more restrictive than in larger cities. Under Canadian law, a court is bound to consider a national average — small communities, as well as large urban centers and rural areas.

As well, Canadian courts will continue to attach importance to the artistic merits of a work. It can reasonably be expected that this will permit most photographic studies of the human nude to escape scrutiny.

Finally, if photographers are accused of violating Canada's obscenity laws, they are entitled to submit evidence of Canadian community standards, such as the rulings of provincial censor boards. Judging from the Towne Cinema Theatres case, this evidence may not be accepted by Canadian courts, but at least consideration must be given to it when it is presented. Such evidence may prove useful to Canadian photographers, especially considering that *Penthouse* magazine currently has the largest newsstand circulation of any magazine in Canada, with 3,500,000 copies sold per month. Its success demonstrates the acceptance of certain types of pornography in the Canadian community and should go a long way in persuading Canadian courts of the legitimacy of most photographers' work.

d. PROHIBITED USES OF OBSCENITY IN CANADA

In Canada, obscenity is governed by both federal and provincial governments. The federal government regulates obscenity by means of the Criminal Code and customs legislation; the provincial governments regulate it by means of statutes establishing censorship boards to classify and regulate the showing of films, or by delegating power to local municipalities to regulate the sale of adult books and magazines.

The federal legislation governs obscenity across the country; provincial legislation regulates obscenity only within the confines of the particular province and you should investigate the regulations that may affect your photographic works.

The primary section in the Criminal Code concerning obscenity is section 163. This section makes it an offense to make, print, publish, distribute, circulate, have in your possession for the purpose of publication, distribution, or circulation, sell, expose to public view, or have in your possession for such a purpose, an obscene photograph. Your motive in committing any of these acts, or your knowledge of the nature or presence of obscene material is not considered.

The definition of obscenity has been part of the Code since 1953, and has survived numerous challenges. However, all of these challenges were made before the Charter of Rights and Freedoms was introduced. It is possible that constitutional challenge to the definition of obscenity may be mounted on the basis of the Charter.

Under section 168 of the Criminal Code, it is an offense to mail anything that is obscene. However, it is not an offense to mail something that might otherwise be considered obscene but concerns a judicial proceeding, a law report, or is in a technical publication intended for circulation among members of the legal or medical professions.

The import of obscene materials into Canada is governed by the Customs Tariff Act. For 117 years, this act gave customs officers a right to seize "immoral and indecent" material at the border. However, in a recent decision of the Federal Court of Appeal, this right was found to be unconstitutional on the basis that it was too vague to be upheld as a reasonable limit on the constitutional right to freedom of expression.

In response, the federal government gave quick passage to a bill to plug the loophole that might have left Canada open to a flood of pornographic material. Parliament passed an amendment to the act to effectively restore to customs officers the power to stop pornography from crossing the border. Customs officials must use the same test Canadian courts use to determine if material is obscene. (See the definition of obscenity in section **a.** above and the previous discussion.)

It should be noted, however, that the amendment to the Customs Tariff Act is a temporary measure, designed to allow the government more time to introduce comprehensive amendments based on the forthcoming recommendations of two parliamentary committees, one studying prostitution and pornography, and the other studying sexual offenses against children and youth.

According to newspaper accounts of the passage of the amendment, a set of instructions has been given to customs inspectors to help them interpret the new law. Based on recent court decisions, the instructions direct customs officers to seize material which shows "sexual acts that appear to degrade or dehumanize any of the participants." This includes scenes of sex in conjunction with violence, submission, or ridicule, whether they are explicit or not, if the material appears to condone or endorse the behavior for pleasure. Scenes of rape, bondage, incest, mutilation, sodomy, buggery, bestiality, necrophilia, and any depiction of people who are, or "apparently are" under 18 years of age in an "even slightly sexually suggestive" context are also prohibited.

Photographers who anticipate bringing into Canada material that might be considered obscene should know that, even though customs officials and the police now share the same definition of obscenity, material found acceptable at the border will not necessary be immune from criminal prosecution.

3
TAKING PHOTOGRAPHS

a. MEETING A PROFESSIONAL STANDARD

Photographers, like other people who provide services, are required by law to meet a certain standard of competence when performing work for others. If they fail to meet that standard, they may be required by a court to pay someone who suffers a loss as a result.

The standard of competence, and the damages that a person who fails to meet it may have to pay, vary with the circumstances. However, a few general rules can be set out.

If you agree to take a photograph, and something goes wrong, you may be found liable either for breach of contract, or for negligence. Generally, you will be found liable if —

(a) you had a duty to live up to a certain standard of conduct,

(b) you breached that duty (i.e., you failed to meet the standard of conduct),

(c) another party suffered damage,

(d) that party's damage was reasonably related to your breach of the duty, and

(e) the party suffering damage did not in some way contributed to the problem, or did not voluntarily assume the risk of a problem occurring.

Let's look at each element.

1. The duty

Your duty to perform competently may arise either in a contract or by some other means. If you have made a contract with someone in which you have agreed to take a photograph, the law assumes a term in that contract that you agreed to meet a certain standard of conduct. The first issue, then, is defining your duty as a photographer.

If you have a contract, and there is a term in that contract specifying the duty of care you will exercise in taking a picture, or there is some representation as to your skill and experience, that term will be used by the court to define the duty.

If, however, your contract does not have a term dealing with duty, the law will have to assume a standard based on the circumstances.

In deciding what duty you should be required to live up to, if any, the court will generally apply the following rule: a person has a duty to perform with the same amount of skill as the average person of the class to which that person belongs or to which that person holds himself or herself as belonging to.

Accordingly, if you represent yourself as a professional photographer, you would have a duty to behave as a professional photographer would. Similarly, if you hold yourself out as an amateur photographer, or someone inexperienced in a certain aspect of photography, a court would impose on you a duty to have in the same way as the average amateur or inexperienced photographer. In deciding what that duty involves, a court would most likely consider how other photographers with the same level of skill as you represented yourself to have would behave in similar circumstances.

2. Breach of duty

Once a court has established the duty to live up to a certain standard of conduct, it then looks to see if you breached that duty. A court will ask, "Did you engage in conduct that involved an unreasonable risk of harm to the other person?" In other words, did you take a recognizable risk that would be sufficient to cause a reasonable person with your experience to hesitate? Did you fail to do something that the average photographer in your position would have ordinarily done? Did you not expect something to occur that the average person in your position would have expected?

The law will not hold you liable if a problem occurs and you could not reasonably have anticipated it. If you have a contract, in such circumstances the law may well consider that your contract has been frustrated; if you do not have a contract, the law will find that you discharged your duty (i.e., that you met the standard of conduct that was required of you).

It is only when you do something that the *reasonable person* would not have done, or fail to do something that the reasonable person would have done, that you will be found liable.

3. Damage

Even though you have failed to live up to the standard of conduct the law imposes on you, a person will succeed in a court action against you only if he or she has suffered damage as a result of your failure. In other words, your liability depends on two elements:

(a) that damage was done, and

(b) that you are the cause of that damage.

The cause of the damage will be discussed in section **4**.

Courts in Canada and the United States approach damages in very different ways. The differences are complicated, but it should be noted that damage awards, in general, are much lower in Canada than in the United States, and that courts in Canada may not award damages for as many kinds of losses as courts in the United States.

The basic determination to be made by every court, whether it be in Canada or the United States, is the kinds of losses which should be compensated, and how much money should be considered as reasonable compensation. The big debate concerns emotional injury where a person's feelings have been hurt because something that is important in an emotional or sentimental sense has been damaged or destroyed.

Another problem courts have been wrestling with is what information should be considered in determining the loss that a party, such as a photographer, has caused someone else. For example, if a photographer ruins pictures of a wedding, how is the loss suffered by the client to be measured? Should it be by the amount of money it cost to hold the wedding, or the cost involved in hiring another choir, minister, church, and photographer to perform the ceremony again?

Neither Canadian nor American courts have resolved these problems definitively. This uncertainty *may* be to a photographer's advantage, in that a person who sues may not be able to recover much money from the photographer. However, it may also be a disadvantage; there is the possibility that someone may be able to recover a significant amount of money.

4. Cause of damage

Even though you may have breached your duty as a photographer, and the person you agreed to take pictures for has suffered, the law will find you liable only if the person's loss arose as a result of your failure. If the loss was caused by some occurrence or consideration that you had nothing to do with and could not reasonably have anticipated, the law will not hold you liable.

5. The other party's conduct

Sometimes a person you agreed to take pictures for may have caused the problem that led to your inability to perform appropriately. The person may be late for an appointment, causing you to rush; he or she may want a photograph taken in a certain location or in a certain manner that you think is technically risky; or he or she may ask you to apply a technique, or use a process, that is very unpredictable.

Alternatively, the other party may have voluntarily assumed the risk of a problem occurring. The person, for example, may have asked you to take a picture in circumstances in which you believe, and have told that person, that problems may arise. Or, you may have informed the person that you are unfamiliar with a certain type of photography or equipment, but you have been asked to take the picture anyway.

In both circumstances, the law may excuse you from liability even though you may have performed poorly and caused the other party damage. In such a case, the court will essentially find that the problem is not your fault — the other party brought it on.

6. Limiting liability

If you do not perform work you have promised to do, or you perform it badly, and if there are no exceptional circumstances, the law will generally find you liable. However, even though you may be found liable, there still are ways to limit, and possibly even eliminate, having to pay damages.

Perhaps the best way is to use a standard contract providing that either you will not be liable in certain circumstances, or that your liability will be limited to a certain sum or to a figure to be calculated in a certain way. The courts will interpret such terms strictly and may in some circumstances refuse to enforce them. However, the use of standard terms can help you in two ways. First, it may discourage some people from suing you, and second, if you are sued, there is always the chance that a court may apply the term of you contract and deny the other party's claim. (**Note:** a standard contract should be prepared by a lawyer.)

Alternatively, if you do not wish to use a contract, or it is inconvenient to do so, make it clear to the person for whom you are taking the pictures what problems, if any, you foresee in doing a job, and your level of skill. If there is some risk associated with a certain technique or pose, say so. If you are unfamiliar with a certain type of equipment that you are asked to use, say so.

Finally, when you point out these things, if at all possible, do it in writing. This will make sure that no misunderstanding arises, and will also provide you with valuable evidence in case the other party sues you.

b. INJURIES IN THE STUDIO OR ON LOCATION

Taking a good photograph requires considerable skill and can sometimes be dangerous. Photographic studios, with electrical wires, darkrooms, and chemical solutions can be a trap for the unwary. Similarly, photographic sets can be very dangerous. A misplaced prop or malfunctioning equipment can injure photographic staff or hired talent.

Perhaps no one can testify to this aspect of photography better than the Larkin brothers. The Larkin brothers were a firm of commercial photographers operating in London, England, in the early years of this century. As one of the city's more accomplished photographic firms, they were hired by an acoustical engineering company to photograph some state of the art speakers the company had recently installed in a movie theater.

Accordingly, the Larkin brothers headed down to the theater with their equipment — a big box camera and plenty of magnesium powder. Magnesium powder was used to produce a flash, as the flash bulb had not yet been developed.

The powder was placed in a metal tray and ignited to produce a brief, but bright fire.

The theater was not the most spacious building, and it was not easy to get a good shot in such cramped surroundings. So, to get the best angle, the Larkins set up the camera on the movie theater stage, in the space between the footlights and the curtain.

In due course, the Larkins ignited their magnesium powder. Unfortunately, owing to the chemical's volatility, it flared up and set the curtain on fire. This started an enormous fire and the theater was badly damaged.

Distraught at this destruction, the theater owner claimed compensation from the acoustics company. The acoustics company then sued the Larkin brothers.

The Court of King's Bench had no hesitation in finding the photographers liable for the damage caused by their flash. It held that the photographers had failed to take proper care, and could not escape liability for the consequences of their failure.

Present photographers are considerably luckier than their predecessors; they are no longer required to use dangerous and unpredictable equipment. However, photography can still be a dangerous business.

Like the Court of King's Bench in the Larkin brothers' case, modern courts in both the United States and Canada have no hesitation in finding photographers liable for the damage suffered by others where such damage is the result of the photographer's lack of care. Photographers find themselves liable for considerable expense. This is especially the case where personal injuries are suffered; both Canadian and American courts have recently awarded increasingly high amounts, often in the hundreds of thousands of dollars, or even millions, to injured victims.

A photographer's liability where damage results from his or her activities is based on the law of negligence. Negligence is generally determined by measuring the action against "what the reasonable man of ordinary prudence would do in the circumstances."

What amounts to negligence depends on the facts of each situation. In an attempt to standardize the court's approach to negligence; however, rules have been developed for certain situations.

One situation involves injuries suffered by a person while on the land or premises of another person. In these cases, the law applies a concept known as "occupier's liability." This standard is that the occupier of land or premises must use reasonable care and skill to ensure that the land or premises do not pose unusual danger to visitors. The occupier may be found liable not only for dangers of which he or she knows, but those of which he or she ought to know. The occupier may be placed under an obligation to take steps to eliminate risks that a reasonable inspection would disclose.

Some jurisdictions have written laws on this standard. The legislation generally does not alter the basic responsibility of the occupier except to make the obligations specifically applicable to certain situations or to enlarge the duty.

Negligence, in general, and occupier's liability, in particular, should be of considerable concern to every professional photographer. The rule applies to any land or premises over which a person has control, whether it is owned or rented, and whether he or she is there on a permanent basis or for a short time.

Accordingly, photographers should ensure that their studios are free from obvious dangers, such as cords or wires that may be tripped over, studios that are poorly lighted, or chemicals that are left around for children or curious visitors to investigate. Photographers should also ensure that location shoots are safe for staff, talent, and any observers.

c. LICENSES AND PROTECTIVE LEGISLATION

1. United States

Various jurisdictions in the United States have made repeated efforts to impose licenses and other requirements on photographers. States that have attempted to require photographers to obtain licenses include Arizona, Florida, Georgia, Hawaii, North Carolina, North Dakota, Tennessee, and Virginia. Typically, these states have enacted legislation or ordinances requiring photographers to obtain a license before being entitled to practice. In some states, photographers are required to write an examination held by a state board of examiners to determine professional confidence, business integrity, and likelihood to contribute to the public good.

In other cases, photographers merely have to pay a license tax if the business is a transient one (i.e., the photographer is a nonresident in a particular jurisdiction.)

These licensing requirements have met with a mixed response from the courts. Generally, legislation or ordinances requiring photographers to pass an examination held by a state board of examiners have been struck down as unconstitutional. The courts have repeatedly ruled that such requirements bear no reasonable relation to the welfare, public health, morals, peace, safety, or comfort of the public generally, and therefore are not within the policing power of the state.

In contrast, legislation or ordinances that merely impose a license on transient photographers have frequently been upheld where the fee imposed is reasonable in size and does not essentially discriminate against nonresidents. However, where the statute does not specifically mention photography, courts on occasion have denied the authority of that jurisdiction to collect a license from photographers.

As well, some legislation imposing licenses on photographers has been struck down by the courts because the license imposed had such a high fee, or was onerous in some other way, that it virtually prevented photographers from conducting business.

The business of taking photographs is taxable as a "privilege" within the meaning of the state provision of the state constitution and is not exempt from license tax on the ground that it is a mechanical pursuit.

Licensing provisions, especially when acted by a municipality, are notoriously difficult to track down. If you wish to conduct business in a state, check with a local attorney to ensure that you have met all requirements that legislation may impose on you.

2. Canada

In Canada, there is no requirement for a photographer to obtain a license. However, photographers are covered by a myriad of laws and regulations that pertain to every business activity. For example, photographers conducting business may be subject to consumer protection legislation, business practices legislation, false and misleading advertising provisions, and zoning regulations.

If you plan to establish a photography business, it would be wise to check with your lawyer to ensure that you have met all of the requirements.

One area that photographers should be especially aware of is tax legislation. There has been some argument in recent years as to whether photographers are subject to sales tax under federal income tax laws. Curiously, these cases have all involved photographers who earn their living by photographing farms from the air and selling such photographs to the farm and homeowners. In all these cases, Canadian courts have decided that the photographers' work was subject to sales tax, and that the photographers were obliged to collect it when their work was sold to a third party. This is the case even when what is sold is actually not a photograph but some variation, such as a painting derived from a photograph.

d. TRESPASSING

Trespass is basically any kind of entry onto the property of another without that person's permission. It can give rise to both criminal and civil liability. Photographers often find it necessary to go on to the property or enter the dwellings of other people to take photographs. Such entry can be illegal where it is made without permission. Accordingly, it is useful to understand the law of trespass.

1. United States

It has been said that "a man's home is his castle," and, for purposes of the law, a person's residence is an impregnable fortress into which no person may enter without the owner's permission.

While this statement may not be accurate under some circumstances, it describes the American law of trespass perfectly. American courts will find a person liable for trespass if he or she intentionally or negligently crosses the boundary onto another's land without the occupant's permission.

In the U.S., trespass is governed by the common law, and may also be covered by state penal codes. In the former case, the land occupier may sue for damages; in the latter case, the state prosecutes, and may, on conviction, impose a fine or term of imprisonment.

American law generally provides that trespass may be committed on or above land. It is committed on land when one enters a building or walks onto property. It is committed over land if one flies or is suspended by some other means over land.

However, in the case of flight by aircraft in the airspace above the land of another, it will only be considered trespass if —

(a) the flight enters into the immediate reaches of the airspace next to the land, and

(b) the flight interferes substantially with the occupant's use and enjoyment of his or her land. The occupier of the land does not have to be on the land at the time of trespass.

Trespass basically involves the violation of another's right to the use and enjoyment of his or her property. However, while use and enjoyment of property are central to trespass, the occupier of the land does not, at the time of the trespass, have to be on the land. In the case of *Ford Motor Co. vs. Williams,* a 1963 Georgia case, it was held that the defendant was liable when he entered into the plaintiff's home, even though the plaintiff was not there at the time.

A variation of the law of trespass that is important to photographers is eavesdropping. Eavesdropping, in most states, is covered by the state penal codes and is an offense punishable by fine or imprisonment. Typically, state codes make it an offense to record a person's actions in a private place without permission, where such record is made with intent "to observe the personal conduct of any other person or persons therein."

In one case, it was held that a photographer should be convicted when he used a hidden camera to secretly photograph young women while they were changing clothes in his attic studio. The court held that it was irrelevant whether or not the photographer saw the person at the moment their picture was taken, or whether he observed the person by means of the photograph.

Not all states use eavesdropping statutes to deal with secret photography. For example, California deals with it as invasion of privacy. For example, in the case of *Dietemann vs. Time, Inc.*, a 1971 California case, it was held that the plaintiff's right to privacy was violated where *Time* reporters entered a woman's home, secretly photographed her, and transmitted conversations by means of a hidden radio to persons outside the house.

The court held that clandestine photography of the woman in her den, and the recording and transmitting of her conversation without consent, resulted in emotional distress that warranted recovery for invasion of privacy in California. In a strongly worded decision, the court stated that the first amendment was not a license to trespass, to steal, or to intrude by electronic means into another's home or office.

The most important defense, and perhaps indeed the only defense to an action for trespass, is consent. If a person expressly or by implication gives permission to another to enter into his or her home, or go onto his or her land, that person cannot later maintain an action for trespass against the person who has acted on such permission.

This principle has interesting application to photography. The main question that arises is whether a photographer who is permitted to enter another's property for a purpose unrelated to photography, commits a trespass when he or she takes a photograph on the property without the landowner's permission.

This is essentially the situation in *Dietemann vs. Time, Inc.*, where the plaintiff permitted reporters with the defendant magazine to enter his home, but for a purpose other than that for which they were actually there. The defendant took the position that the plaintiff had consented to their presence, and accordingly there could be no trespass. The court rejected this defense, saying that even though one invites others into one's home, one takes a risk that visitors may not be what they seem. Despite the fact that visitors may repeat all they hear and observe when they leave, the plaintiff should not be required to take the risk that what the visitors heard and saw would be transmitted by photograph or radio to the public at large or to any segment of it that the visitors might select.

Another case in point is *Rawls vs. Conde Nast Publications Inc.*, a 1971 Florida decision. In that case, employees of the defendant magazine publisher entered the plaintiff's house without her permission and, in her absence, and believing that they had her permission, began to photograph its contents and a model in various parts of it. The plaintiff returned home, and upon finding the defendant's employees photographing in her house, made no meaningful effort to remove them, and demonstrated no visible emotional distress; instead, she acquiesced in their continued presence. On these facts, the court found that there had been no invasion of her privacy.

It should be noted that consent to photograph can be revoked. If it is revoked before publication of photographs that have been taken without consent has occurred, publication may not occur.

It should also be noted that consent obtained by fraud is no consent at all.

2. Canada

It was a hot evening, that August 24, 1963, as Pierre Massue looked through the peep hole in the door of his Montreal apartment. Massue was president of a private investigation company which had been retained by a man to find out if his wife was cheating on him. The man believed his wife was seeing one Laurent Hebert. Massue rented an apartment across the hall from Hebert so that he could watch, through the peep hole, Hebert's every move.

One night, Massue believed that he could catch Hebert in the act. And so, at 4:25 a.m., Massue entered Hebert's apartment to take incriminating pictures.

Unfortunately for Massue, things did not work out as planned. Not only was his client's wife in the apartment, but Hebert and two other men were there as well. None of the occupants took kindly to the investigator's presence; a fight ensued, and Massue was forcibly ejected.

Subsequently, Massue was charged with breaking and entering a place with intent to commit an indictable offense, contrary to the Criminal Code. He was duly convicted.

As the Massue case indicates, photographers often find it necessary to go on to the property or enter the dwellings of other people to obtain photographs. Such entry can be illegal where it is made without the occupant's permission. Accordingly, it is useful to understand the law of trespass.

Trespass is basically any kind of entry onto the property of another without that person's permission. It can give rise to both criminal and civil liability.

The relevant sections of the Criminal Code that legislate trespass are as follows:

Section 430(1) provides that —

everyone commits mischief who willfully

c. obstructs, interrupts, or interferes with the lawful use, enjoyment or operation of property; or

d. obstructs, interrupts, or interferes with any person in the lawful enjoyment or operation of property.

Section 177 provides that —

everyone who, without lawful excuse, the proof of which lies upon him, loiters or prowls at night upon the property of another person near a dwelling house situated on that property is guilty of an offense...

It should be noted that an offense under section 177 can only be committed at night (which has been defined in the Code as between 9:00 p.m. and 6:00 a.m.) and only upon another person's property. Someone who loiters or prowls upon their own property or in the street is not guilty of trespassing at night.

Civil liability for trespassing arises both by means of the common law and, in some provinces, by means of provincial statutes specifically creating the offense of petty trespass. Provincial trespass statutes typically provide that anyone who unlawfully enters, or in any other way trespasses upon another's land that is enclosed, that is a garden or lawn, or that has on it a sign prohibiting trespassing, is guilty of an offense.

The common law, on the other hand, imposes prohibitions that are not as precise as those set out in provincial trespass statutes. The common law basically provides that a person trespasses upon land if he or she —

(a) enters upon land in the possession of another, or

(b) remains upon such land, or projects or places any object upon it, without lawful justification.

The most common form of trespass is, of course, physical entry by a person onto land, or into a building, occupied by another person. In common law the slightest crossing of a boundary is sufficient. For example, if you put your hand through a window, or sit upon a fence, you may be trespassing. It is not necessary for a person to be forbidden from entering upon the property for trespass to occur; it is sufficient that the person is permitted to enter upon the property for one purpose, but enters upon it for a different purpose.

For example, if you were permitted to enter a shopping center to shop, you may be trespassing if you enter for the purpose of photographing window displays or people shopping. Other examples could be entering theaters, art galleries, or museums.

It is not trespassing to fly over another person's land. It might well be trespassing though if you suspend yourself

58

over someone's land by some other means (for example, by climbing out on the bough of a tree, or by suspending yourself from a crane).

e. HARASSMENT

1. United States

Few people in public life have been photographed as frequently as Jacqueline Onassis. The widow of former president John F. Kennedy, the widow of a Greek tycoon, and a prominent American socialite in her own right, Onassis is a permanent player on the public stage.

Her prominence has been considerably assisted by photography; indeed, one individual, Ronald E. Galella, has made a virtual career out of photographing her.

Publicity has placed a considerable burden on Jacqueline Onassis, who is practically unable to go out in public without having her picture taken. She and members of her family are consistently subjected to public scrutiny. Her situation creates a fundamental dilemma for American law. The courts must balance her right to privacy and peace of mind against the American public's enduring interest in her conduct as a public figure.

These competing values were pitted against each other in the case between Galella and Onassis. That case is the leading decision on harassment in the United States and was decided in 1973.

The case arose when Ronald Galella attempted to photograph John Kennedy as the boy rode his bicycle in Central Park across from the Kennedy home. Galella had jumped into the boy's path, and so alarmed Secret Service agents protecting the boy that they laid a complaint against him.

Galella was arrested, charged, and subsequently acquitted. Following his acquittal, Galella sued the agents and

Onassis, alleging false arrest, malicious prosecution, and interference with trade. Onassis countered by suing Galella for invasion of privacy, assault, battery, intentional infliction of emotional distress, and harassment.

Prior to the trial, the parties reached an agreement whereby Galella agreed not to engage in further photographic exploits until the issues between them had been resolved. But Galella did not observe the agreement, and a temporary restraining order to prevent further harassment of Onassis and her children was issued. Within two months, Galella was charged with violating the order; and a new order was signed requiring the photographer to keep 100 yards from the Onassis apartment and 50 yards from Onassis and her children. Surveillance was also prohibited.

Eventually, the matter came to trial; six full weeks of testimony and argument were heard. The evidence disclosed that Galella —

> had on occasion intentionally, physically touched Mrs. Onassis and her daughter, caused fear of physical contact in his frenzied attempts to get their pictures, followed the defendant and her children too closely in an automobile, endangered the safety of the children while they were swimming, waterskiing, and horseback riding.

In the words of the trial court, Galella had "insinuated himself into the very fabric of Mrs. Onassis' life."

The court, dismissed Galella's complaint and upheld Onassis' complaint. Galella appealed, and succeeded in having the trial court's order modified. He still had strict guidelines concerning his conduct and actions, and was not allowed within 25 feet of Onassis, or 30 feet of her children, but he was in a position to continue his photography.

The Galella decision is a milestone in photography and the law. It confirms the court's power to control and restrain photographers in their pursuit of otherwise lawful activity. At the same time, however, it implies that photographers, even in the most extreme circumstances, should retain their right to take pictures in a limited capacity.

As the New York Court of Appeals itself said:

> ...legitimate countervailing social needs may warrant some intrusion despite some of an individual's reasonable expectation of privacy and freedom of harassment. However, the interference allowed may be no greater than that necessary to protect the overriding public interest.

The Galella case is undoubtedly the most important authority on this issue, and will guide not only the courts of New York, but other states as well, for many years to come. However, it is not the only applicable law. Many states, including New York, provide in their state penal codes that harassment is a criminal offense. The New York penal law, for example, makes it a crime when, with intent to harass, a person follows another in a public place, inflicts physical contact, or engages in any annoying conduct without legitimate cause.

It has also repeatedly been held that conduct sufficient to evoke criminal liability for harassment may be the basis to private action. Accordingly, photographers whose activities might well be held to violate the penal code of their state could be exposing themselves not only to criminal prosecution, but to a civil action with financial penalties as well.

The Galella case is, of course, an extreme example. Apart from the type of conduct described in it, American courts will generally be reluctant to find harassment has occurred, especially where the activity complained of has occurred in a public place. It has been held, for example, that it is no invasion of privacy to follow a person about and watch him or her. Neither is it an invasion of privacy to take a person's photograph in such circumstances, since this amounts to nothing more than recording what a person would be free to see if they were on the scene. These principles have been well established in numerous cases concerning private detectives and police whose work frequently involves the surveillance of suspects.

2. Canada

As noted earlier in this book, you are generally free to take a photograph of a person in a public place. However, Canadian law does impose a limit on the extent to which you can go to take someone's picture in such circumstances. If you surpass these limits, you may be charged with harassment.

If you follow someone or watch a person for the purpose of compelling that person to do something or not to do something that they would otherwise be free to do, you are harassing. But if you wait around someone's house to take a picture, you could be excused on the basis that the taking of a photograph might be considered "obtaining or communicating information," which does not fall under the definition of harassment.

The law concerning harassment is much stricter when the situation involves the Queen. The Criminal Code provides that:

anyone who willfully, in the presence of Her Majesty,

a. does an act with intent to alarm Her Majesty or to break public peace; or

b. does an act that is intended or is likely to cause bodily harm to Her Majesty,

is guilty of an indictable offense and is liable to imprisonment for 14 years.

No convictions under this section have been reported recently, and so it is difficult to determine how this section would be applied. However, given the vagueness of the wording, and the general principle underlying it, which is to protect the Queen from unreasonable approaches, a photographer who is overly aggressive in an attempt to take a picture of the Queen runs considerable risk of being charged under this section.

Also, there is a catch-all provision in the Criminal Code concerning harassment (section 175). This section provides that everyone who causes a disturbance in or near a public place by impending or molesting another person, or by loitering and in any way obstructing persons who are there, commits an offense. This section has typically been applied against people who make unreasonable noise or impede the flow of pedestrians in a public place, but there is no reason why it could not be applied against a photographer who is unreasonably persistent in attempting to take the picture of a person in a public place.

Harassment is also covered by the common law. Canadian courts have been reluctant, in the absence of statutory provisions such as those discussed above, to limit the extent to which a person can watch or follow another in public. However, in certain circumstances the courts will find a person liable who behaves in such a manner.

In the few Canadian cases on harassment, courts have relied on nuisance laws as a basis for their decisions. The leading example is a 1957 Ontario decision.

In that case, the plaintiffs, who operated a boat in Toronto Harbour, sued the defendants, who were in the charge of the Toronto Harbour Police, after the police followed their boat continuously for three months. The police believed that the defendants were operating a water taxi without a license, and had followed them in an attempt to prove their suspicion.

The Ontario High Court of Justice had no difficulty in finding that the behavior of the Harbour Police was unreasonable, and it granted the plaintiffs an injunction and $2,000 in damages.

This case sets out several tests for harassment:

(a) The effect of the conduct complained of on the average reasonable man

63

(b) Whether that conduct is something more than mere personal inconvenience

(c) Whether the conduct is an interference with the enjoyment of a person's quiet and personal freedom

(d) Whether it is something that discomposes or injuriously affects the senses or the nerves

None of these tests is precise; no doubt to permit flexibility in their application. These tests do oblige a photographer, however, to consider the effect of his or her actions on the party he or she is attempting to photograph. If the attempt to take a picture, and the photographer's conduct, is such that it would interfere with personal freedom or would upset the subject, it is possible a lawsuit in nuisance might occur.

Photographers should also be aware of the willingness of Canadian courts to grant damages to parties who become so distressed by the deliberate and annoying conduct of another that they suffer physical harm. The leading case on this issue occurred in 1897 in England. In that case, Downton, as a practical joke, told Wilkinson that her husband had had both his legs broken in an accident. This information was false, and Wilkinson suffered such nervous shock that she became violently ill. She sued Downton for the injuries she had suffered. The court found that Downton had willfully done an act calculated to cause physical harm to Wilkinson — that is, to infringe her legal right to person safety — and had in fact caused her physical harm.

Although the Wilkinson case has nothing to do with photography, it is a warning for all those who, in an attempt to take another's photograph, act in such a way that it is reasonably likely that the subject would become upset or ill. The Wilkinson case suggests that there are definite limits on the extent to which a photographer can go in attempting to take another's photograph, apart from any question of nuisance or trespass.

f. THE RIGHT TO PRIVACY

If you are like most people, you probably do not mind being photographed when you are ready for it, and when you know who is taking the picture and why. But you do not like being taken by surprise or being photographed by strangers; it violates your sense of privacy and your desire to be left alone.

Many people take their privacy very seriously. They build walls around their houses, hire bodyguards to keep photographers at bay, or take legal action against those who take their picture. Because privacy is so important to many people, it is essential that every photographer understand the rights and obligations inherent in it.

Privacy, in a legal sense, can refer to different things. It can refer to an intrusion upon a person's solitude or seclusion, such as when a photographer follows a person, or looks through a window, to take that person's picture. Or it can refer to an appropriation of a person's image for commercial purposes, such as when a celebrity's picture is used to promote a product.

These two concepts of privacy are quite distinct, and accordingly, they have been dealt with in different sections of this book. The first is discussed in this chapter; the second, in chapter 4.

Can someone forbid you from taking his or her picture, even when you are not trespassing or harassing? In other words, does that person have the right to privacy which can be enforced against you?

1. United States

If you were to judge from the law alone, it seems that the United States is a nation obsessed with privacy. The right to privacy is one of the most discussed, and most quickly developing concepts in American law.

The right to privacy really embraces two different concepts. It refers to the right to be left alone, to enjoy one's seclusion or solitude. It also refers, however, to the right to control the use of one's image for commercial purposes. These two concepts are quite distinct, and accordingly, the former is discussed in this section, while the latter is discussed in chapter 4.

The right to privacy is truly an American invention. It is the creation of two American writers, Samuel D. Warren, and Louis D. Brandelis, who, in 1890, published an article in the Harvard Law Review which suggested that the growing excesses of the press made it necessary for American law to extend protection to private individuals from the unjustifiable infliction of mental suffering.

In an era of yellow journalism, the suggestion of a right to privacy found quick favor. In the same year the article appeared, a New York judge allowed recovery on the independent basis of the right of privacy where an actress had appeared on the stage in tights, and without her permission, had her picture taken by the defendant.

The concept really caught on in 1902, however, as a result of a case in New York. In that case, the Rochester Folding Box Company used a woman's picture, without her consent, to advertise its product. The court concluded that the woman had no right to action because there was no principle in law known to them that would allow her to recover damages, and because a recognition of any legal right to obtain damages would lead to a long lawsuit.

This decision outraged the public. As a result, in the very next session of the legislature, privacy laws were enacted.

Several states have either adopted legislation similar to the New York civil rights law, or, by means of common-law decision, have recognized the right to privacy.

The New York statute provides as follows:

(a) A person, firm or corporation that uses for advertising purposes, or for the purposes of trade, the name, portrait or picture of any living person without having first obtained the written consent of such person, or if a minor of his or her parent or guardian, is guilty of a misdemeanor.

(b) Any person whose name, portrait, or picture is used for advertising purposes or for the purposes of trade without his or her written consent having been first obtained may maintain an action in the Supreme Court of New York against whoever uses his name, portrait, or picture.

These two sections are deceptively short and simple. The question of what is a use of a portrait or picture for advertising purposes or for the purposes of trade has given rise to many lawsuits and to the development of certain guiding principles.

First, American courts have long held that if a newspaper or television station takes a person's picture in connection with a news item, then the use of the picture does not fall under the definition of a picture being used for trade or advertising purposes. However, while not preventing the use of photographs in connection with news items, the courts have imposed definite restrictions on the news media and their attempts to obtain photographs.

Basing their decision on the right to privacy, American courts have held that a person will be liable if he or she intrudes on another's privacy in such a way as would be offensive or objectionable to a reasonable person. For example, it has been held to be an invasion of the right to privacy where a hospital patient is photographed in a hospital bed, or where a person is photographed in the seclusion of his or her home.

Photographs taken in public places pose a special difficulty for American courts. On one hand, in a public place everyone present may see what is occurring and a photographer who takes a picture of this scene does no more than record something that everyone is already viewing. However, it is still possible in some circumstances for a person's dignity to be violated. Accordingly, courts have decided that even in a public place there can still be some things which are private. For example, in the case of *Daily Times Democrat vs. Graham*, a 1964 Alabama case, the court held that a woman in a "fun house" whose dress unexpectedly was blown up had her right of privacy violated when she was photographed in such circumstances. However, other American courts have not been so quick to find a right of action. In the case of *Neff vs. Time*, a 1976 Pennsylvania case, the court found that the plaintiff's right to privacy had not been violated when the defendant news magazine ran a photograph depicting the plaintiff, at a public event, with the zipper of his trousers open.

It is also an invasion of privacy when a photograph is taken or made by means of bribery or other inducement.

Apart from these limitations, American law does not place much restriction on photographers who take pictures in ways that cannot be considered trespass or harassment. Where a picture is taken on the street or in a public place, such as a courtroom or sporting event, the courts have traditionally declined to consider such situations an invasion of privacy. This has held true even though the photography may disturb the person whose picture is being taken.

For example, in the 1948 Minneapolis case of *Berg vs. Minneapolis Star & Tribune Co.*, the court held that a newspaper photographer did not violate the plaintiff's right to privacy by taking, despite the plaintiff's objections, a photograph of him in a courtroom.

In a case with similar facts, *United States vs. Gugle*, it was said that the operation of a camera is a lawful act and a citizen's privilege to take pictures, unless made specifically unlawful by statute, is a civil right protected by the American Constitution.

Similarly, in *Forster vs. Manchester*, a 1963 Pennsylvania case, it was held that the plaintiff's right to privacy was not violated when a private detective, who had been hired by an insurer of a driver with whom the plaintiff had been involved in an automobile accident, took motion pictures of her. The pictures were taken on public streets, and because of this, the court concluded that by going to public places, the plaintiff had exposed herself to public observation, and therefore was not entitled to an extensive right of privacy.

2. Canada

Traditionally, Canadian courts have been reluctant to recognize a general right to privacy. This can be seen from two cases — neither of them Canadian, but both good law in Canada.

The first is *Victoria Park Raceway and Recreational Grounds Co. Ltd. vs. Taylor*, a 1937 decision of the High Court of Australia.

In that case, the owner of land across the street from a raceway built a platform high enough to give a perfect view of the plaintiff's raceway. He then permitted a local radio station to put an announcer on top of the platform, and broadcast the races. As a result of the station's broadcast, the raceway owner's business dropped considerably, no doubt because people were unwilling to pay for what they could get from the radio station for free.

The raceway owner sought a permanent injunction to prevent the land from being used in this way, alleging that such use was unreasonable, that it was an interference with the use and enjoyment of his own land, and that it violated his right of privacy.

The High Court of Australia rejected the raceway owner's claim. The Chief of Justice, speaking for the Court, stated that he was:

> unable to see that any right of the plaintiff has been violated or any wrong done to him. Any person is entitled to look over the plaintiff's fences and to see what goes on in the plaintiff's land…The defendant does no wrong to the plaintiff by looking at what takes place on the plaintiff's land. Further, he does no wrong to the plaintiff by describing to other persons, to as wide an audience as he can obtain, what takes place on the plaintiff's grounds … However desirable some limitation upon invasions of privacy might be, no authority was cited which shows that any general right of privacy exists.

In support of its conclusion, the court cited an 1861 English case in which it had been decided that:

> with regard to the question of privacy, no doubt the owner of a house would prefer that a neighbor should not have the right of looking into his windows or yard, but neither this court nor a court of law will interfere on the mere ground of invasion of privacy; and a party has a right even to open new windows although he is thereby enabled to overlook his neighbor's premises, and so interfering, perhaps, with his comfort.

The other leading case in this regard is *Bernstein of Leigh (Baron) vs. Skyviews and General Ltd.*, a 1977 case decided in England. An English baron owned an estate named Coppings Farm in Kent. Photographers from an aerophotography company took a single aerial photograph of Lord Bernstein's country house as part of their business of taking aerial photographs of all types of properties and selling them to the owners. Lord Bernstein, however, was not in a buying mood, and complained that photographing his house without permission was a gross invasion of privacy. In due course, he sued the company for damages.

Ironically, Lord Bernstein was, at the time, the Chairman of Granada Television, a company which had recently made a series of educational films called "The Land." To make the films, helicopters flew all over England and photographed the land below, all without the consent of the property owners. It was this, as well as an exhaustive analysis of previous cases, that made the court decide in favor of the aerial photography company:

> there is ... no law against taking a photograph, and the mere taking of a photograph cannot turn an act which is not a trespass into the plaintiff's air space into one that is a trespass.

It noted that Lord Bernstein's counsel was unable to cite any principle of law or authority which would entitle him to prevent someone taking a photograph of his property for an innocent purpose, provided that they did not commit some other tort such as trespass or nuisance in doing so.

The court cautioned, however, that it did not want its judgment to be understood as meaning that under no circumstances could a successful action be brought against an aerial photographer to restrain his or her activities. It said that while:

> no court would regard the taking of a single photograph as an actionable nuisance ... if the circumstances were such that a plaintiff was subjected to harassment of constant surveillance of his house from the air, accompanied by the photographing of his every activity, I am far from saying that the court would not regard such a monstrous invasion of his privacy as an actionable nuisance for which they would give relief.

However, there are signs that the law may be changing. Three provinces (Saskatchewan, British Columbia, and Manitoba) have enacted privacy statutes. These statutes use different language but set out a common principle. The Saskatchewan Privacy Act, for example, provides that where there has been "auditory or visual surveillance of a person by any means including eavesdropping, watching, spying, besetting, or following, and whether or not accomplished by trespass" without the express or implied consent of a person, it is a violation of that person's privacy. This general principle is qualified, however, by another section which states that —

> the nature and degree of privacy to which a person is entitled in any situation or in relation to any situation or matter is that which is reasonable in the circumstances, due regard being given to the lawful interests of others.

In considering what is reasonable, the Saskatchewan courts consider a number of factors, including the nature, incidents, and occasion of the act, conduct or publication, and the effect on the health and welfare, or the social business or financial position, of the person and his or her family or relatives.

The Saskatchewan statute further provides that an act is not a violation of privacy where it was committed by a person engaged in news gathering for a newspaper or other paper containing public news, or a licensed broadcaster, and the act was reasonable in the circumstances and was necessary for or incidental to ordinary news gathering activities. Nor is it considered to be an act of violation of privacy where there were reasonable grounds for belief that the matter published was of public interest or was fair comment on a matter of public interest.

As well, some decisions in provinces that do not have privacy laws suggest that a right to privacy does exist. However, all of these cases involve annoying telephone calls, and do not concern photography; accordingly, it cannot accurately be predicted what effect these decisions will have on Canadian law where privacy and photography is concerned.

You could probably presume with reasonable safety that you are entitled to take a picture of another person or his or her property, so long as you do not trespass upon the property, or act in a persistent and annoying manner. You could, for example, photograph your neighbors from your own property; photograph a celebrity as he or she emerged from a restaurant or theater; or take a picture of a person on the street, whether or not you are forbidden to do so. The law in such circumstances will not prevent the photograph from being taken, so long as the manner in which the photograph was taken is not objectionable.

4
USING PHOTOGRAPHS

a. ADVERTISEMENTS

1. United States

Bubble gum is something that few people think about twice. But in 1953, bubble gum was at the center of a lawsuit that demonstrates how important the commercial use of a personality can be, and how critical it is for photographers to recognize this right and act accordingly.

In this case, a bubble gum manufacturer sued a competitor for invasion of the exclusive right to use photographs of a leading baseball player in connection with the sale of bubble gum. The defending company had induced the same player to authorize the use of his picture in connection with the sale of its gum during the term of the first company's contract with him. The court ruled in favor of the original contract on the basis that the player had the right to grant the use of his picture, and he, or the recipient of such a grant, was entitled to prevent violation of that right. The court stated:

> We think that in addition and independent of that right of privacy (which in New York derives from statute), a man has a right in the publicity value of his photograph, i.e., the right to grant the exclusive privilege of publishing his picture, and that such a grant may be validly made "in gross," i.e., without any accompanying transfer of a business or of anything else.

Whether publicity value is labelled a "property" right is immaterial, for here, as often elsewhere, the tag "property" simply symbolizes the fact that courts enforce a claim which has pecuniary value.

This right might be called "a right of publicity." It is common knowledge that many prominent persons (especially actors and ball players), far from having their feelings bruised through public exposure of their likenesses, would feel sorely deprived if they no longer received money for authorizing advertisements popularizing their countenances, displayed in newspapers, magazines, buses, trains, and subways. This right of publicity would usually yield them no money unless it could be made the subject of an exclusive grant which barred any other advertiser from using their pictures.

Appropriation of personality should be a major concern for all photographers who do commercial work of any kind. Almost all prominent entertainers and athletes exploit their images to full commercial potential. Endorsement of products, appearances in advertisements, and participation in promotions of all kinds constitute an important source of income for most celebrities.

The appropriation of personality has become an important feature of privacy law in most states. Several states have enacted right to privacy statutes, while many others rely on the common law.

Those states that have enacted privacy statutes governing the appropriation of personality have generally modelled their legislation on New York's statute. The New York right of privacy law was the first privacy statute enacted in the U.S. and is the most succinctly phrased.

In summary, the law basically provides that a person, firm or corporation that uses for advertising purposes, or for the purposes of trade, the name, portrait or picture of any living person without having first obtained the written consent of such person, or, if a minor, of his or her parent or guardian, is guilty of a misdemeanor. If unauthorized use is made, the person whose name, portrait, or picture is used may obtain an injunction to prevent further use and sue for damages.

However, professional photographers are permitted to exhibit their work in their places of business unless specifically prohibited by their subjects. Further, anyone is allowed to use the name, portrait, or picture of the manufacturer or dealer in connection with products they have produced or sold. And anyone may use the name, portrait, or picture of an author, composer, or artist in connection with a work he or she has sold.

Many of the states that have not enacted privacy statutes have followed the same general principles as those set out in the New York statute.

The purpose of the New York provisions is to protect the individual from another's selfish commercial exploitation of his or her personality. Protection is generally considered a right personal to the subject depicted in an item of advertising or promotion; it has generally been held to cease upon the individual's death (although this is not necessarily the case where the individual has, during his or her lifetime, merchandised his or her personality, and made agreements for the continuation of such merchandising following death).

The main issue that arises in applying these principles is determining what constitutes "use" for advertising purposes. This issue was faced by the New York courts in 1937 in an action brought by a professional Hindu musician as a result of the publication of a story in the local newspaper about a rope trick that he performed for his living. A picture of the man performing his trick had been used to illustrate the story, and he sued on the basis that his privacy had been violated by the picture's publication. The court, in holding that his right of privacy had not been violated, set out four rules concerning the use of photographs as illustrations for articles. These rules have been applied by American courts in several states since then and provide a useful guide for discussion.

The rules have been summarized in an article by Judge Hofstadler of the New York Supreme Court as follows:

(a) Recovery under New York's Right of Privacy Statute may be obtained if the photograph is published in or is part of an advertisement or for advertising purposes.

(b) Recovery may be obtained if the photograph is used in connection with a work of fiction.

(c) No recovery may be had if the photograph is published in connection with an article of current news or immediate public interest.

(d) No recovery may be had as a general rule if the article is educational or informative in character.

Let us discuss each of the uses referred to in Judge Hofstadler's summary in turn.

(a) Advertising purposes

Within the meaning of the New York statute, an advertiser who uses a person's name, portrait, or picture for advertising purposes is seeking that person's patronage for a particular service or product.

In order to be liable, the advertiser must have intended to use that person's name, picture, or likeness to capitalize on the name, identity, or acts.

It's not enough, however, for a person's name, portrait, or picture to merely appear in an advertisement; the picture must be recognizable from the advertisement itself as referring to that person, and the use in the advertisement must be more than incidental.

A question that American courts are frequently called on to answer is whether a photograph used by a newspaper or magazine to promote itself is used for "advertising purposes." Typically, this situation arises when a magazine or newspaper takes a photograph of a famous event or person, prints it as a news item, and then, at a later date, reproduces it in an advertisement for the publication.

An example of this occurred in the case of *Namath vs. Sports Illustrated*, a 1975 New York case. The defendant magazine ran several stories on Joe Namath, a famous athlete. To illustrate these stories, it used several photographs of him. The magazine then published promotional materials to stimulate subscriptions, which used Namath's picture as an illustration. Namath sued, alleging that his right of privacy had been violated because his picture had been used for advertising purposes.

Both the Trial and Appeal courts ruled in the magazine's favor. The court reached this decision on the basis that the use of his photograph was entirely incidental to the magazine's advertising, and that the language of the advertisement did not suggest that Namath had endorsed *Sports Illustrated*.

The Namath case has been followed by many other courts. Generally, as long as an advertisement is not designed in such a way that a person whose photograph is used in it appears to be endorsing the publication in which the advertisement appears, and as long as the photograph has been previously used as a legitimate news item, the publication may safely use the person's photograph.

The American justice system is reluctant to encroach upon the freedom of the press, so publications have no difficulty using people's photographs to promote their sales. While it's difficult to see how freedom of the press would be limited, the principle has probably become too well entrenched to dislodge.

Several other principles have been developed by the courts for determining when a person's portrait or picture has been used for advertising purposes. While the rules discussed above concern what constitutes an advertising purpose, these principles concern what will be considered "use for material."

First, some meaningful or purposeful commercial use of a person's portrait or picture is essential in order to sue for invasion of privacy. For example, it was held in the *Moglen vs. Varsity Pajamas Inc.*, a 1961 New York case, that a clothing manufacturer who had reproduced, on fabric, torn-out portions of a newspaper, including an article dealing with a player in a particular tennis match, did not violate the tennis player's right to privacy.

Second, the person must be clearly identifiable in a photograph used for advertising purposes if that person's right to privacy is to be considered violated. If no one other than that person can identify the picture, the person has really suffered no loss, and no right of privacy has been violated.

Third, and finally, a person's picture must be used in more than an isolated manner to be an invasion of privacy. Thus, it would not be a violation of a person's right to privacy if a person was photographed as one of the crowd, or among a group of spectators at a public event.

Note also that where a person has signed a consent permitting another to use his or her photograph for advertising purposes, but discovers that the photograph is being used for a different advertising purpose, that person will not generally be able to claim an invasion of privacy. Instead, American courts have generally dealt with such situations as contractual matters. The court will look at the terms of the consent given, the use of the photograph actually made, and award damages for breach of contract if that use does not come within the terms of consent.

(b) Works of fiction

It has been long held by American courts that statutes such as New York's right of privacy law permit a person whose photograph has been used in a work of fiction be compensated for violation of right of privacy. Fiction has been held to include not only pure fantasy, but fictional versions of current news or of past events of legitimate public or general interest, and even of accounts which by reason of inaccuracy, falsehood, or distortion are, in actuality, untrue. However, courts have been somewhat hesitant to uphold that right where a person's picture is used in honest error.

(c) News and other items of public interest

The news media probably use more photographs than all other forms of communications combined. With the number of newspapers, news magazines, and television outlets in the United States, and the number of different stories appearing in them every day, the number of photographs used in any given year probably is in the millions.

For this reason, there are many court cases based on privacy statutes arising from the use of photographs with news articles or other items of public interest. Because there are so many privacy cases, American courts quickly set out principles pertaining to privacy and news, and have adhered to them virtually without variation ever since.

The basic principle established by American courts is that it is not a violation of a person's right to privacy if the person's photograph or portrait is used in connection with an article of current news or immediate public interest. This rule applies not only to printed materials but to television broadcasts as well.

This principle is based upon the view that a person's right of privacy, at least to the extent of permitting a limited scrutiny, comes second to the public interest in obtaining information, especially where the subject of the inquiry has the status of a "public figure."

Application of this principle has led to some unusual, but logical, results. These decisions suggest that American courts tend to interpret the news and item of current interest exception to the right of privacy in a broad manner. Indeed, it could actually be said that the public's right to know and be informed about the activities of public figures is practically absolute unless commercialization can be conclusively demonstrated.

Perhaps the most bizarre application of this principle occurred in the case of *Paulsen vs. Personality Posters Inc.*, a 1968 New York case. Pat Paulsen was a well-known television comedian, who, in 1968, conducted a mock campaign for the presidency. As part of his campaign, he created a parody of an old campaign photograph. The court described this parody as follows:

> soulfully expressioned plaintiff attired in beruffled cap and prim frock, in a style which might best be characterized as "latter-day Edna May Oliver," is shown holding an unlit candle in one hand while his other arm cradles a rubber tire which is hoisted onto his right shoulder. A contemporary touch is added by a banner rigged across the plaintiff's chest in the manner, if not with the style, of a beauty contestant, which bears the legend "1968."

Paulsen's agent sent a copy of this photograph to the defendant company, apparently with the intention of negotiating a license agreement for its distribution as a poster. Several months after receiving the photograph, the defendant, on its own volition and without the plaintiff's permission, printed up copies of a poster depicting the plaintiff's photograph and bearing the words "For President" at the bottom of the page.

Paulsen had undertaken an extensive merchandising program in which he conveyed an exclusive license to a California company in connection with buttons, stickers, and posters relating to the "Pat Paulsen for President" campaign. Believing that the company's distribution of its posters infringed upon and interfered with this license arrangement,

Paulsen attempted to persuade the company to stop distributing the poster. The company refused, and so Paulsen sued, alleging invasion of his right of privacy.

The Supreme Court of New York held that the right of privacy law was not intended to limit activities involving dissemination of news or information concerning matters of local interest. News and information activities should be considered privileged and outside of the "purposes of trade" contemplated by the statute, even though they are also carried on for profit. In its view, the legitimate interest of the public should not be limited to dissemination of news, in the sense of current events, but should be extended to embrace all types of factual, educational, and historical data, or even entertainment and amusement concerning interesting phases of human activity in general. Paulsen's campaign was newsworthy: he was a well-known public personality who by choice actively promoted and stimulated public attention, and he had projected himself into the national political scene. In denying Paulsen's claim, the court bluntly stated —

> limitations upon the permissible in political expression are almost non-existent. It is the strength of our political system that it can survive and flourish in such matrix, where the sensibilities of the participants must bow to the superior public interest in completely unfettered and unabridged free discussion of whatever persuasion, merit or style.

Another interesting case involved an action for damages brought by the parents of an eight-year-old boy who had been kidnapped and murdered. The plaintiff's son disappeared from his Sioux City, Iowa, home, and remained missing for approximately one month until September 29, 1954, when his mutilated and decomposed body was discovered in a field outside of town. That evening, the *Journal Tribune* newspaper carried on its front page a picture of the site where the body was found and the boy's decaying remains. The boy's parents sued the newspaper for violation of their right to privacy, alleging that they suffered untold mental anguish and humiliation as a result of the publication of a picture of their son's body. The Supreme Court of Iowa held that the newspaper publisher was not liable to the boy's parents for invasion of their right to privacy because the boy's disappearance and death was a "top rank news story" and, thus, a matter of legitimate public interest. The publication of photographs in connection with matters of public interest could, as a general rule, not give rise to an action for violation of one's right to privacy.

A final interesting case is that of *Abernathy vs. Thornton*, a 1955 Alabama case. In that case, a photograph of a murdered body showing the metal bullet protruding from the victim's head was published. The court held that publication of this photograph was not a violation of the plaintiff's right of privacy because

> there can be no privacy in that which is already public. It does not exist in the dissemination of news and news events...

The court's approach to privacy and news has been well summed up in a 1951 Pennsylvania decision, *Leverton vs. Curtis Publishing Co.* In that case, the facts of which are given later in this chapter, the court stated:

> the plaintiff says the picture is simply sensational, which it also is, but the courts are not concerned with the canons of good taste, and pictures which startle, shock, and even horrify may be freely published, provided they are not libelous or indecent, if the subject of the picture consents, or if the occasion is such that his right of privacy does not protect him from the publication.

However, there are limits to the type of photographs American courts will allow to be published under the guise of news or items of public interest. The test which is typically applied is not the currency of the publication in which the picture appears, but whether the picture is illustrative of a matter of legitimate public interest. While most courts have found that, for the purposes of establishing limits to the right of privacy, the public's interest in information is almost limitless and insatiable, a line can be drawn in rare cases. Some material is not acceptable.

A leading example is the case of *Leverton vs. Curtis Publishing Co.*, referred to above. Eleanor Leverton, a child, had been photographed by a newspaper reporter as she lay in the street immediately after being struck by an automobile. The newspaper then ran the photograph. Almost two years later, Curtis Publishing Co. used the photograph as an illustration for an article on pedestrian carelessness entitled "They Asked To Be Killed." Leverton sued Curtis for violation of her right to privacy. The court decided in favor of Leverton on the basis that the use of a photograph to illustrate an article unrelated to the particular accident was not newsworthy and could not, therefore, be published under the exception for news and items of public interest. In addition, it was decided that the publication of the photograph offended the sensibilities of the ordinary person.

A similar case is that of *Metzger vs. Dell Publishing Co.*, a 1955 New York case. Metzger, together with some other young people, had their photograph used in connection with a magazine story related to youth gangs. The plaintiffs were not shown to have any connection with any gang of any sort, but they had orally consented to the taking of their picture. The plaintiffs sued for violation of their right to privacy. In granting judgment in their favor, the court noted that while it was legitimate to discuss the existence of gangs and gangsters, the photograph of the young people could not be considered to be newsworthy because there was no connection between it and information set out in the story.

The difficulty facing American courts in situations such as the two discussed above, is determining whether a photograph and a story with which it appears can be considered newsworthy. If the story is newsworthy, and if there is some general relationship between the story and the plaintiff, the courts will hold that publication of the plaintiff's photograph cannot be considered a violation of his or her right of privacy. Thus, in *Delinger vs. American News Co.*, a 1958 New York case, a magazine article illustrated by a photograph of Delinger, a physical training instructor, as a candidate for the title of Mr. Universe 1956, was published. The article contained only a general discussion of the relationship between muscular development and virility, and did not constitute a violation of the plaintiff's right to privacy.

Similarly, in *Oma vs. Hillman Periodicals, Inc.*, a 1953 New York decision, it was held not to be a violation of privacy where the plaintiff, a professional boxer, had his photograph published on the cover of the defendant's magazine beneath the headline reading "Tycoon — This Man Can Make $25,000 On A Single Deal, But It Might Cost Him His Life. Why?"

From these cases and others, it would appear that the constitutional right of free speech is applied in a very generous manner, so that a person's picture may be published in connection with an item of news or public interest, so long as there is some actual connection between the article and the person, and the article is newsworthy.

(d) Educational or informative articles

It has long been the law that, as a general rule, articles which are not strictly news but satisfy educational needs, such as stories of distant places, tales of historical personages and events, and reproductions of items of past news, are treated in the same manner as items of news or current public interest, for the purposes of limiting the right to privacy.

2.   Canada

In everyday life, a personality is thought of as a combination of many things. It is considered to be a bundle of qualities, such as a person's appearance, mannerisms, voice, and behavior. All of them are unique to a particular person and define who that person is.

But in law, personality has a special and more precise meaning. It refers to a select few qualities that are capable of imitation or appropriation, such as voice or appearance.

In recent years, the legal meaning of personality has come under increasing scrutiny as more and more actions are brought in Canadian courts alleging "appropriation of personality." Typically, in these cases, someone claims that some aspect of his or her personality has been taken and used for commercial purposes without permission. Usually it is the person's image that is used, in the form of a photograph, to advertise a product.

In one case, a professional water-skier with an international reputation, who had a distinctive photograph of himself waterskiing that he used for commercial purposes, sued the operator of a summer camp for appropriation of personality. In attempts to attract business to the camp, the operator had the water skier's photograph copied and published as a line drawing in a brochure publicizing the camp. The skier's name did not appear in the brochure, but the drawing would have been recognizable to a small circle of knowledgeable persons.

The court ruled in favor of the water skier; it considered that the reproduction of the photograph for commercial advantage was an invasion of the skier's exclusive right to market his personality. Accordingly, it awarded him damages based on the amount he ought reasonably to have received in the market for permission to publish the drawings, which in this case came to $500.

The novelty of appropriation of personality cases poses some difficulty for photographers in Canada. There is really no legal guidance as to what activity is permitted and what is not. However, four provinces have enacted privacy laws that generally consider use of a person's name or likeness for the purpose of advertising, promotion, or trade, without that person's consent, to be a violation of privacy.

While these statutes represent a bold new step for Canadian law, there have been no decisions based on them, and accordingly, photographers in Canada are left with only cautious and general support for the concept of appropriation of personality. To be prudent, you should ensure that you either obtain releases from subjects whose portraits you intend to use for commercial purposes, or ensure that your photographs are not used for commercial purposes.

The difficulty for photographers is determining what constitutes a commercial purpose. As Canadian law offers no guidance whatsoever, apart from the statutes, it is suggested that you take guidance from American law, which suggests, in brief, that a commercial purpose embraces virtually all types of promotional endeavors, except those that involve as their main object the communication of news or information on matters of public interest.

b. NEWS

Virtually every professional photographer has sold a picture to a newspaper, news magazine, or TV outlet. Indeed, the mass media may well be the biggest consumer of pictures the average photographer has. Accordingly, it is important to be aware of the limitations on the use of photographs in a news context.

1. United States

American courts have traditionally held the view that the publication of photographs is not a violation of anyone's legal right to privacy as long as they are used in connection with an article of current news or immediate public interest. This approach is based on the view that the public has an interest in the free dissemination of news, and as a result, the ability of the mass media to gather and publish information should not be restricted except in the most extreme circumstances.

The Walters case, which involved the murder of a young girl and subsequent news story, is an excellent illustration of this attitude.

A 14-year-old Georgia girl was abducted and murdered, and her body wrapped in chains and thrown into a river. A Georgia newspaper published photographs, which were taken at close range, showing the decomposition of part of the child's body, and the chains wrapped around it.

The girl's mother sued the newspaper for invasion of her right to privacy. In her petition, she alleged that the newspaper had overstepped the bounds of acceptable news coverage.

Unfortunately for the girl's mother, both the trial court and the Supreme Court of Georgia took a different view. The Supreme Court stated:

> where an incident is a matter of public interest, or the subject matter of a public investigation, a publication in connection therewith can be a violation of no one's legal right of privacy…there are many instances of grief and human suffering which the law cannot redress. The present case is one of those instances. Through no fault of the petitioner or her deceased child, they became the objects of widespread public interest…the dissemination of information pertaining thereto would not amount to a violation of the petitioner's right to privacy.

Much of the history of the right to privacy has been concerned with the definition of such "extreme circumstances." After literally hundreds of decisions on the issue, some of which have gone all the way to the Supreme Court, a few principles have emerged.

First, a photograph illustrating an article on a matter of public interest will not be considered to have violated the right to privacy unless the photograph has no real relationship to the article, or unless the article is an advertisement in disguise.

A good illustration of this principle is the case of *L. Murray vs. New York Magazine Company*, a 1967 New York case.

The plaintiff was a newspaper vendor in Queens County. Every year he attended the St. Patrick's Day Parade in Manhattan dressed in an Irish costume — an Irish hat, green bow tie, and green pin. He was not of Irish extraction, but enjoyed participating in the festivities.

Mr. Murray's colorful garb did not escape attention. While watching the parade, he was photographed without his consent, by a freelance photographer who then sold the picture to *New York Magazine*.

Two years later, the magazine ran Murray's picture on its front cover beneath a headline promoting a feature article entitled "The Last of the Irish Immigrants," by Jimmy Breslin. Murray was not named in the article or on the cover.

Murray sued for breach of his right of privacy under section 51 of New York's civil rights law. The New York Court of Appeal found in favor of the magazine. It pointed out that the article dealt with a matter of public interest; that the photograph had been used to highlight a newsworthy event; that Murray had been singled out and photographed only because his presence constituted a visual participation in a public event that invited special attention; and that Murray's photograph was reasonably related to the subject matter of the article.

Second, photography or other information may not be used in news in such a way as to place the persons depicted in a false light. However, to be held liable, the person publishing such false news must have published it with knowledge of its falseness with reckless disregard for the truth.

This principle was enunciated in the case of *Time, Inc. vs. Hill*, a 1967 decision of the U.S. Supreme Court.

In 1952, the quiet residential neighborhood of Whitemarsh, Pennsylvania, was invaded by three escaped convicts. The convicts entered the home of James J. Hill, and took him, his wife, and his two children hostage for 19 terrifying hours. It was a sensational crime, and attracted a great deal of media interest. After the ordeal had ended, Hill received many offers from TV stations and magazines offering to buy the rights to the story. Hill, however, was unwilling to expose his family to further publicity, and rejected all of the offers.

Several months after the incident, Joseph Hayes published a novel about the incident, *The Desperate Hours*. The book was generally based on the Hill family's experiences, but also contained several elements of pure fiction. Subsequently, the novel was made into a play, which reproduced the same fictional aspects.

When the play based on the book began its opening run, *Life* magazine published an article on it. It arranged to have the Hills' Whitemarsh house made available for photos, and took members of the cast to the house and photographed them in scenes from the play. These photographs, together with a story, appeared in *Life* magazine's February 28, 1955 issue under the heading "True Crime Inspires Tense Play."

The family had not consented to *Life* magazine's publication of its story, and sued for breach of their right of privacy under the New York right to privacy law. The Hill family maintained that *Life* magazine had deliberately fictionalized the original event for commercial purposes, and that neither the play or *Life*'s story was a "true account" of what had happened so as to bring it within the first principle discussed above. *Life*, on the other hand, took the position that the article was legitimate news coverage, and fair comment on a matter of public interest.

The case went all the way to the U.S. Supreme Court. By a five-to-four vote, the court held that *Life* magazine's story should be considered privileged, unless it was found that it made the false statements with knowledge of falsity or reckless disregard of the truth.

With this ruling the court brought the libel rule it had laid down in *New York Times vs. Sullivan* into the field of invasion of privacy actions involving the press and public persons.

The U.S. Supreme Court emphasized that the Hill family were public persons, having been catapulted into the news by dramatic and unforeseen events, and were thus "in the public domain" insofar as their activities and experiences were concerned. As Mr. Justice Douglas put it,

> such privacy as a person normally has ceases when his life has ceased to be private.

A third and final principle developed by the courts to deal with privacy and the news concerns the unwarranted publicity of truth. In such cases, a court will award damages to a person where the news media has published revelations that are so intimate and so unwarranted as to outrage the community's notion of decency.

Photographers should also be aware of the possibility that photographs, or more often, photographs published in connection with cut lines or stories, could be defamatory. The law of defamation is very complicated and highly developed. Suffice it to say that a photograph or other publication will be considered defamatory if it tends to lower a person in the estimation of others. This could be a statement or other form of information that brings the person into hatred, contempt, or ridicule, and it may be achieved by direct means or by irony, caricature, or some other way.

American law has developed a number of defenses to publication of a defamatory statement, such as truth, privilege, and fair comment. These defenses are continually evolving and reflect the continuous tug and pull that goes on between the media and members of the public whose affairs are held up to public scrutiny.

Whenever publishing a picture, a photographer should take care to ensure that the subject of the picture is correctly identified, and that the facts in a cut line or story are reasonably believed to be true and have been properly investigated.

Another consideration for photographers wishing to use photographs in a news context is the law of copyright. Section 113(c) of the Copyright Act provides that —

> in the case of a work lawfully reproduced in useful articles that have been offered for sale or other distribution to the public, copyright does not include any right to the making, distribution, or display of pictures, or photographs of such articles in connection with advertisements or commentaries related to the distribution or display of such articles, or in connection with news reports.

Thus, where a copyright work has been reproduced in a useful article, and that article has been offered for sale to the public, it will not be a breach of copyright in that work to publish a picture of the article in which it appears in the context of a news report. This section of the Copyright Act specifically reverses the usual role that copying in a different medium constitutes infringement.

Another section of the Copyright Act relevant to the use of photographs concerns "fair use." It provides that it is not an infringement of copyright to make fair use of a work by reproducing it for purposes of criticism, comment, or news reporting. (See chapter 6 for more on copyright.)

Photographers should note that educational or informative articles are generally treated in the same way as news stories. It has long been the law that articles that are not strictly news but satisfy educational needs, such as stories of distant places and tales of historical personages and events, are treated in the same manner, for the purposes of limiting the right to privacy.

However, works of fiction are very different. A person whose photograph is used in a work of fiction may sue for violation of his or her right to privacy. Fiction includes not only pure fantasy, but fictionalized versions of current news or past events of legitimate public interest, and even of accounts which by reason of inaccuracy, falsehood, or distortion are untrue. (However, courts have been hesitant in the last instance where a person's picture has appeared as a result of an honest error by a publication attempting to provide its readers with an account of a newsworthy situation.)

2. Canada

Fortunately for photographers, there are few limitations on using photographs for news under Canadian law.

In Canada privacy laws have not developed to any great extent, so there is virtually no reported case law dealing with the relationship between privacy and the use of photographs in news. Indeed, with the recent enactment of the Charter of Rights and Freedoms, which makes freedom of the press and other media of communication a fundamental right of all Canadians, it can be expected that limitations on photographs used for news will continue to be minimal.

There are, however, a few restrictions which photographers should remember. In addition to the restrictions on photographing court proceedings, official secrets, currency, and buildings (see chapter 1), there are restrictions dealing with false news, criminal libel, copyright, and civil libel.

(a) False news

The Criminal Code contains two sections that deal with the presentation of false news. The first, section 372(1), provides that —

> everyone, who with intent to injure or alarm any person, conveys or causes or procures to be conveyed by letter, telegram, telephone, cable, radio, or otherwise, information that

he knows is false is guilty of an indictable offense and is liable to imprisonment for two years.

This section should apply where a news medium published a parody or spoof or ran a false story to generate some useful response. However, even in these circumstances, it would have to be established that the news medium *intended* to injure or alarm a person.

Section 181 of the Code provides that —

everyone who willfully publishes a statement, tale or news that he knows is false and that causes or is likely to cause injury or mischief to a public interest is guilty of an indictable offense and is liable to imprisonment for two years.

This section could also apply in the case of a parody or spoof or planting a false story. However, this section also requires that intent be established and that the published material be false.

Neither applies where a news medium innocently publishes something that, in fact, is not true. However, while the news medium in this case would be protected from criminal liability, it might be subject to a civil action, such as an action for libel or violation of copyright (see sections (c) and (d) below).

(b) Criminal libel

Section 301 of the Criminal code provides that —

everyone who publishes a defamatory libel is guilty of an indictable offense and is liable to imprisonment for two years.

The punishment for publishing defamatory libel increases to five years where the publisher knows that the material is false.

Defamatory libel is defined as something published without lawful justification that is likely to injure the reputation of a person by exposing that person to hatred, contempt, or ridicule, or by insulting them.

94

While criminal libel generally pertains to the written or spoken word, it may also apply to photographs.

The law of libel is very complicated, and is not set out in detail here. However, it should be noted that the primary defenses to a defamatory libel charge are truth, fair comment, and privilege, as provided in the Criminal Code. Of these, the most important to a photographer is likely to be truth. For example, if you took a picture that showed a person in an embarrassing situation, and consequently held that person to ridicule, you might well be able to argue that the picture merely depicted what was actually occurring. However, this defense might not apply if a false impression of a situation was conveyed by the use of light and shadow or photographic distortion.

(c) Copyright

Copyright is covered thoroughly in chapter 6. It is important at this point, however, to note that while great liberties have been extended to the media, such liberties do not include relief from the application of copyright law. Even though a news medium may publish a picture for news purposes, it may not, in doing so, violate copyright in that picture held by another.

Determining whether publication of a photograph has violated someone's copyright is not a simple matter. In the case of a single photograph, the copyright owner must give permission before publication. However, it is not an infringement of copyright where there is "fair dealing" with a work for the purposes of private study, research, criticism, review, or newspaper summary.

In the case of a book of photographs that is summarized by a newspaper or reviewed by some other mass medium, it is possible that selections of photographs from the book may be reproduced without violating the author's copyright. Similarly, in the case of a photographic exhibit, certain pictures could be reproduced in connection with a review of the exhibit without infringing on copyright. It should be noted, though, if too many photographs are reproduced, then the review may no longer be fair use of the exhibits photographs.

(d) Civil libel

Libel may give rise to criminal action, as noted above, or a civil action. The tests and defenses in both cases are similar. The consequences, however, are quite different. In the case of criminal libel, a guilty party may be imprisoned; in civil libel, a guilty party will merely have to pay damages.

In a criminal libel, a definition of the offense is set out in the Criminal Code; with civil libel, however, there is no precise definition, as it has merely evolved through judicial decisions.

Libel is essentially a false statement about a person — a statement that degrades the person in the eyes of other citizens and exposes him or her to hatred, contempt, or ridicule.

A "false statement" includes virtually every permanent form of expression, including photographs. A photograph may constitute a libel in several ways. First, it may depict a situation falsely through the use of light and shadow, optical techniques, or deliberate or accidental distortion or alteration. Alternatively, the picture may be true, but may be accompanied by a false statement. Or the statement could be true, but because of the manner in which it is expressed, still be libelous. These latter cases are far more common than the former.

In one case, a newspaper published a picture of an infant in connection with a charity drive. Underneath the picture the words "This girl was helped by the community chest three years, and the normal life she leads today is a result of your contributions back in 1949. But there are others, like Mary in the story below. Why not help her too?" Then followed a history of the girl, describing in detail her un-happy life.

The photograph of the infant had been published without her parents' knowledge or consent. The parents sued for libel, alleging that the statement that their daughter had received public assistance was defamatory. On appeal, the court held that the article was libelous, notwithstanding the good intent and good purpose with which it was published.

c. IN COURT

1. General

Photographs play an important role in today's judicial system. While photographs can be used in many different court situations, they must be taken and introduced as evidence with great care. Because of photography's ability to provoke emotional responses, a few rules of thumb will help ensure that your pictures meet the court requirements.

(a) When taking a photograph, note the time of day the picture was taken, the weather and light conditions, your location, the camera settings, and the lenses used.

(b) When shooting the location, try to shoot under the same circumstances as when the crime, or problem, is alleged to have occurred. For example, if you are shooting an accident scene where it was alleged that a tree obscured a traffic sign, the photograph should be taken in the same season, and preferably in the same month, as when the accident occurred.

(c) When taking pictures of people, such as accident or murder victims, avoid recording emotional expressions on their faces if possible. Emotional expressions are frequently used as grounds for excluding a photograph as evidence because they may arouse the jury. If your subject is dead, it is, of course, impossible to do anything about the expression. The most you can do in this circumstance is confine yourself to as objective and undramatic a record as you are able to produce.

(d) Avoid lenses, perspectives, or developing techniques that might distort the picture. In particular, avoid methods that might distort critical aspects of a scene, such as the color of the objects, the distance between objects, the size of objects, and the relationship of objects with other things surrounding them.

(e) Shoot a variety of pictures of a scene showing the context in which an object appears. If photographing a wound, for example, shoot the wound itself, the limb on which it appears, and then the whole body. This serves two purposes. First, while one photograph may be unacceptable to a court, another might be accepted, and your effort might still prove useful. Second, you will allow viewers to have a better idea of an object of injury.

(f) Be careful about the quality of your photographs. Courts have occasionally excluded photographs from evidence because they are so poor they distort the conditions depicted in them.

(g) Be careful about colored and enlarged photographs. While such photographs have generally been viewed as admissible evidence provided they represent the scene or object depicted with substantial accuracy, there is a danger that they will be considered as an inexact reproduction or prejudicial to the case.

(h) Ensure that your equipment is working properly. One of the reasons photographs are often admitted is because the process by which they are taken is generally very reliable. If this reliability cannot be established, however, the photograph produced may be cast in doubt. Accordingly, when taking photographs you reasonably expect will be used in court, check your equipment to ensure that it is working properly. For the experienced photographer, this may seem unnecessary; however, it will allow you, if called upon to testify, to state that you did check the accuracy of your equipment, and that you are confident the picture produced is a reliable presentation of the scene depicted in it.

These rules apply to both Canadian and U.S. courts. You should note, however, that Canadian courts tend to be more conservative than U.S. courts. Also, in Canada, there are various pieces of legislation concerning the use of photographs of documents and other business records. Because of their narrow application, these rules have been omitted here. If the photograph of a document is important in a case, however, these acts should be considered.

2. United States

It was May 27, 1920, and the baseball game at Boss Field in Evansville, Indiana, was in full swing. Among the many spectators watching the game was 11-year-old Alfred Lee Price. Alfred loved baseball, but this was to be the last game he would ever watch. For in one of the most bizarre athletic accidents ever recorded, Alfred was hit on the head with a baseball, and died in the hospital two days later.

Alfred's father, Alfred Sr., sued the game's organizers for the wrongful death of his son.

During the trial, his lawyer persuaded the court to accept into evidence a photograph of Alfred lying in a casket after preparation by a mortician and prior to interment. The photograph, the lawyer successfully argued, should be accepted on the basis that it showed Alfred Jr.'s physical characteristics and corroborated testimony that Alfred Jr. was a "nice looking and healthy chap," and it established the fact that the boy's parent incurred funeral expenses for him, and that "he was properly interred."

It was a powerful photograph, and the court no doubt found it so: the jury awarded Alfred Sr. $14,500 in damages, and the court rendered the judgment on the verdict.

The defendant, the Evansville School Corporation, was outraged. In its view, the photograph's submission was completely unacceptable. It appealed the judgment.

On appeal, the Appellate Court of Indiana was also moved by the photograph — so moved, in fact, that it reversed the judgment, ordered a new trial, and gave a decision in which it found the photograph's introduction to be a fundamental error. In its opinion, the photograph "was immaterial and irrelevant to any of the material facts, in issue, and was prejudicial to the defendant."

The lawyers had a duty to present relevant and material facts to the jury, and to introduce evidence solely for the purpose of arousing the passions and prejudices of the jury, and in such a manner as to cause them to abandon any serious consideration of the facts of the case and give expression only to their emotions, is clearly outside the scope of such duty.

The Evansville case, as it has come to be known, is probably the most famous decision on the use of photographs in court. It established that, while photographs can be very useful in the judicial process, there are definite limits to their use.

Since that time, U.S. courts have struggled to determine how and when photographs should be used at trial. The results of this search, despite the condemnation photographic evidence received in the Evansville case, have been an increasing reliance on photographs in judicial decision making. Photographers have brought their special skills to bear on an ever-widening variety of situations:

- A worker fell from a scaffold after a plank broke, and the Appellate Court of Illinois allowed photographs of the allegedly defective scaffolding to be introduced as evidence. The photographs showed knots that, in the position of witnesses viewing them, were sufficient to cause the plank's breakage.

- Twenty-eight photographs of a murder victim showing bruises to her body, wounds caused by strangulation, and the effects of repeated stabbing, were admitted by the Appellate Court of Arizona in the trial of a man accused of causing the woman's death. In admitting the photographs, the Court said,

  > gruesome photographs may be admitted to corroborate the State's theory of whether and how the crime was committed, to identify the deceased, to show the location of mortal wounds, and to aid the jury in understanding testimony.

- An Ohio court admitted five graphic photos of a murder victim, which were taken at both the burial scene and the autopsy room to support forensic evidence concerning commission of aggravated murder by the accused.

- In an action for damage alleged to have been caused to a bean crop growing on a farmer's land by chemical spraying, the Supreme Court of Oregon admitted photographs of the damaged crop as evidence of the condition of the crop after it was sprayed.

- In a dispute over the boundary line between two parties' land, the Supreme Court of Kansas admitted photographs of the land in dispute.

- In a case against Sears, Roebuck & Co. for damages suffered when two of their "Road Handler" tires blew out, an Indiana Court admitted photographs of the tires showing the damage.

- In a motor vehicle accident case, an Indiana court admitted photographs of the plaintiff's vehicle that showed blood on its white roof. In the court's view, the photographs were relevant evidence of head injuries sustained by the plaintiff in the collision.

- A carpenter was hit in the eye when the head came off a defective nail as he was hammering it. The carpenter sued the nail manufacturer and a Washington court admitted photographs taken with an electron microscope showing magnification of the nail head lodged in the eye.

With the burgeoning use of photographs in court, the law has developed a number of guidelines concerning their introduction into evidence and use at trial.

(a) Photographs as graphic portrayals of oral testimony

Most courts view photographs as merely graphic portrayals of oral testimony. They will admit photographs only where some witness has testified that the photograph depicts certain things he or she personally observed. This witness need not be the photographer, or someone who knows something of the conditions or manner of the photograph's creation. This person need only be familiar with the facts depicted in the photograph. As a result, it is rare that the photograph itself will be evidence; it will merely function as an illustration of a witness's oral testimony.

(b) Photographs as reliable records of a scene

However, some courts are now viewing photographs as "silent witnesses," (i.e., a form of testimony that speaks for itself, and whose trustworthiness is based not on comparison with the person who has taken an oath and thereafter describes a scene, but on the reliability of the photographic process).

Where a court takes this approach, there is no need for a witness to testify that the photograph depicts certain things personally observed; all that is needed is testimony concerning the process by which the photograph was produced.

The different approaches taken by the courts on the use of photographs have two results for photographers. First, courts taking the graphic portrayal of oral testimony approach will offer fewer opportunities for photographs to be used in court, since the entire contents of the photograph have to be verified by oral testimony.

Second, the photographers may be personally involved in the trial to varying degrees, depending on which approach is taken. If the former approach is taken, a photographer may not be called upon to testify at all; if the latter approach is taken, a photographer will likely be an important part of the process by which the photograph's admissibility is established.

Further, these rules must be observed:

(a) A photograph must be accurate and correctly portray what it purports to show. Such portrayal must be without distortion or other distractions.

(b) The photograph must be helpful in understanding the facts relevant to the matter. Relevancy is determined by an inquiry into whether or not a witness would be permitted to describe the objects or scene photographed.

(c) The photograph should not be of such a character as to divert the minds of the jury to improper or irrelevant considerations, or to arouse their passions and prejudices in such a manner as to cause them to abandon any serious consideration of the facts of the case and give expression only to their emotions. Photographs that are prohibited by this rule may be excluded by the trial judge.

(d) Where a photograph depicts a posed or artificially reconstructed scene, it must go no further than to portray the positions of persons and objects as reflected in undisputed testimony. Where a photograph portrays only the version of the facts supported by one party's witnesses, the courts will frequently refuse to admit them into evidence, because of the danger that the jury will confuse the reconstruction with objective facts.

3. Canada

Mrs. Nisnick entered the witness box limping and using a cane; her court appearance was obviously a painful experience for her. Mrs. Nisnick had been injured in an automobile accident and was seeking damages for her injuries. The court had already found the other party to blame and was now hearing evidence as to the extent of her loss.

Mrs. Nisnick testified that her injuries were so severe that she could not walk without the help of a cane. Her job as a saleswoman had also been affected because she could not move around the store without holding on to something. When asked to describe her mobility, she replied, "I can walk, but it is under tormenting pain." As she spoke these words, Mrs. Nisnick was not aware of the evidence the courtroom would hear next. But had she known, she might have chosen her words with greater care — for the trial was to be transformed from an ordinary personal injury case into one of the most embarrassing and humiliating moments of her life.

The surprise was simple but effective — and almost entirely due to the power of photography. It consisted of eight clips of film taken by a private investigator; it showed Mrs. Nisnick doing everything she said she could not do. The film showed her getting in and out of her car, walking through a shopping plaza to the store where she worked, window shopping as she went, and modelling a coat for a customer while at work — all without a limp or a cane.

Mrs. Nisnick, no doubt, was shocked, and so was the court; it awarded the defendant all of the expenses incurred by it in preparing and showing the film and deducted this amount from Mrs. Nisnick's award. The court also reserved some extraordinarily harsh words for Mrs. Nisnick:

it is shocking to see such an attempted abuse of the process of the courts and such a deliberate effort to perpetrate a fraud upon this court ...

The presiding judge declared,

I am unable to give any credence to her evidence. Throughout it, she grossly exaggerated her ills; the story of the cane is shown to be a pure fabrication of her imagination and not worthy of belief.

The Nisnick case is but one example of the important role photography plays in the judicial process today. Some other examples indicate how large a role this can be:

- In a New Brunswick case, a diabetic woman was charged with having murdered the child she was entrusted to babysit by injecting it with insulin. Photographs taken of the baby a few months before its death were admitted to show its healthy condition prior to its death.

- In the Supreme Court of Canada case of *Draper vs. Jocklyn*, the court was called upon to determine the amount of damage an accident victim should receive. The court admitted pictures of the defendant which showed two wires, used to hold fractured bones in place, protruding from his face. The court decided that the photographs accurately and unemotionally depicted the treatment the plaintiff had had to endure as a result of his injuries, and since such treatment was relevant to the calculation of damages, the photographs were relevant and admissible.

- "Topographical" photographs, showing the physical environment in which a murder victim was found, were admitted by the Prince Edward Island Supreme Court in the trial of the two people accused of murder.

- The Nova Scotia Court of Appeal admitted color photographs of a victim's bruised, lacerated, and bloody face and body in the trial of the victim's assailant.

- The Manitoba Queen's Bench admitted photographs of documents in a negligence case, where the original documents had been lost. The photographs enabled the plaintiff to establish several key points in the case.

- In an action by a manufacturing company for an injunction to prohibit a competitor from using confidential information acquired from a former employee of the company, the British Columbia Court of Appeal permitted the company to take photographs of the competitor's products to help it determine whether the competitor had used secrets obtained from the plaintiff.

- In a lawsuit brought against the Labatt Brewing Company by a man who allegedly lost his sight in one eye when a bottle of the brewery's beer exploded and sent glass into his face, the court permitted the plaintiff to photograph the brewery's premises to document its manufacturing processes.

- In a paternity suit, the Ontario Unified Family Court permitted the introduction of photographs of the man holding the child as evidence that he was its father.

Several Canadian courts have admitted photographs of the mutilated or even burned remains of a murder victim. The most unique situation occurred in *R. vs. Bannister*, a 1936 murder case in which the court admitted photographs of the charred remains of the victim as they appeared at the time of a postmortem examination.

While photographs can be used in many different court situations, they must be taken and introduced as evidence, with great care. Because of photography's ability to provoke emotional responses, and because scenes can be photographically altered so easily, the courts have laid down strict rules concerning the use of pictures in judicial proceedings.

The most relevant of these rules, from a photographer's perspective, can be summarized as follows:

(a) A photograph must be accurate in the sense that it truly depicts what it purports to depict.

(b) A photograph must be fair in the sense that it is not misleading or intended to mislead.

(c) A photograph cannot be introduced into court as evidence unless testimony is first given which proves that the qualities referred to in the first two rules exist. This testimony should usually be given by the photographer and the processor, but this does not always have to be the case. Accordingly, photographers taking pictures for use in court should be prepared to testify.

(d) Even when these conditions have been met, and before the photograph may be introduced into court as evidence, the trial judge must be satisfied that it is not so inflammatory as to unduly prejudice the fair trial of a party.

d. PHOTOGRAPHIC COMPETITIONS

Every photographer likes to have his or her work given the recognition it deserves. One of the main sources of recognition is photography awards given by magazines in contests, and in photographic competitions run by camera clubs, art galleries, and the like.

Photographic contests and competitions are good for all involved. Budding photographers receive a higher profile for their work, the public is exposed to a wider variety of photographic work than they might otherwise see, and the contest sponsors are able to bring a higher profile to themselves and the art of photography. However, anyone involved in photography contests or competitions should consider several issues.

One of the most important considerations is the subsequent use of photographs entered in contests and competitions. A magazine or camera club will frequently want to publish winning entries; they may even use them in advertisements for their magazine or club, as the case may be. However, other participants in contests may not want such widespread circulation to occur. Accordingly, the subsequent uses of a photograph should be clearly stated. If they are not, photographers submitting work should find out exactly what uses are involved, and prohibit or negotiate any uses they consider to be questionable.

Unless a magazine or camera club clearly states that it may publish a winning photograph or use it for commercial purposes, it is questionable, both in the United States and Canada, whether they are permitted to do so. Widespread publication of a photograph is one of the most important rights a photographer has. A photographer may reasonably take the position that such publication may not occur without permission unless the contest rules set out that that will be the case.

Another important consideration is ownership of the photograph. The photographer may own the negative to a picture, but, by virtue of the relationship to a person in the photograph, the photographer may not be able to reproduce it without the subject's permission. If, for example, the person has paid a photographer to take his or her picture, the photographer may not be entitled to do anything with that photograph except with the permission of the person who paid for it. The photographer may be entitled to retain the negative, but this does not automatically convey the right to reproduce the negative.

A final consideration is copyright. Publishing a photograph without a copyright notice may jeopardize both domestic and international rights in some circumstances. Accordingly, photographers submitting work, and magazines printing it, should be careful to place a copyright notice on or around the photograph to ensure that all available rights are preserved. Copyright is discussed in greater detail in chapter 6.

5
RELEASES

a. WHAT IS A RELEASE?

A release is the written consent of a person to have his or her picture used by another. It is called a release because the person giving it releases the person taking the photograph from liability as long as the photograph is used in accordance with the release's conditions. A release often sets out the types of use which may be made of a photograph, the persons who are permitted to make such use, and the payment, if any, that is made in return for the release being given.

If the photographer gives something of value to his or her subject in return for obtaining the right to use the subject's picture, the law views the release as a contract. Similarly, if the release has a "seal" (which is generally a red paper wafer purchased from a stationer, rather than an actual wax seal) affixed to it beside the signatures, the law will again view the release as a contract, even though the photographer has given nothing of value to the other party.

Traditionally, courts have required an exchange of something of value (or "consideration" in legal language) for a contract to be effective. However, they have also traditionally made an exception in cases where the parties affixed a seal near their signatures. Centuries ago, a seal connoted an agreement of great importance, and over the years has come to be of such significance that no consideration is required where one is used on a contractual document.

If, however, no consideration is given in return for permission to use the photograph, and no seals are used on the contract, the release will be judged a mere license. Unless a release specifies that it is irrevocable, it can be revoked at any time by the person giving it, even though the photographer may have gone to considerable expense in preparing the photograph.

The difference between these different types of release can be critical, as an unfortunate New York doctor discovered. In that case, a well-known New York personality had signed a release permitting a company, owned by the doctor, to use her name on a perfume it had developed.

That release read as follows:

> I am pleased to give you herewith permission to use my name and portrait in connection with the perfume which you have originated, known as the Perfume Mary Garden.

Relying on the release, the company marketed the perfume, and went to considerable expense promoting it. Twenty years later, the plaintiff decided to revoke the release, and sued to prevent the defendant from continuing its use of her name. The court decided in her favor.

The judge reached this conclusion because he considered the release to be a gratuitous license, revocable at any time even though action had been taken on it.

b. WHEN SHOULD YOU OBTAIN A RELEASE?

You do not generally need a release to *take* someone's picture; you are generally free to take another person's picture whether that person agrees or not. However, a photographer may need a release to *use* someone's picture. The law gives a person the right to control the use of his or her picture. Specifically, a person's picture may not be used for purposes of trade or advertising without permission.

Accordingly, you need to obtain a release when you believe that you are likely to use someone's picture for a commercial purpose, and in particular for purposes of trade or advertising. If you are taking the picture solely for personal use, a release is not necessary.

It is often difficult to predict what use you will make of a particular photograph. You may intend at the time you take it to use it for purely personal purposes, but later you realize that it could be put to some commercial use. It is important to remember that it is not your *intention* at the time you take the picture that determines whether a release is necessary; it is the *purpose* to which the picture is actually put. If at any time the photograph is used for commercial purposes, the question of whether or not the subject in the picture gave permission for the photograph to be so used will arise.

It is better to err on the side of caution and obtain a release if there is a remote possibility that the picture could be put to commercial use.

In speaking of "commercial use," or "for purposes of trade or advertising," it should be noted that such uses do not include news, or use in court. Such uses have long been considered by both American and Canadian law to be so important that they have consistently held that permission need not be obtained from a person whose picture is used for these purposes.

A release may not be necessary for certain other uses. Specifically, a release may not be needed for —

(a) a professional photographer's exhibition of work in his or her place of business, unless the subject objects in writing;

(b) use of the photograph of a manufacturer or dealer in goods, in connection with the sale of goods of that manufacturer or dealer; or

(c) use of the photograph of an artist, composer or author in connection with the sale of their work.

However, these exceptions apply only in states that have a right to privacy statute that includes a term to this effect. For example, under New York's privacy law says that —

> Nothing contained in this act shall be so construed as to prevent any person, firm, or corporation, practicing the profession of photography, from exhibiting in or about his or its establishment specimens of the work of such establishment, unless the same is continued by such person, firm, or corporation after written notice objecting thereto has been given by the person portrayed; and nothing contained in this act shall be so construed as to prevent any person, firm, or corporation from using the name, portrait or picture of any manufacturer or dealer in connection with the goods, wares and merchandise manufactured, produced or dealt in by him which he has sold or disposed of with such name, portrait or picture used in connection therewith; or from using the name, portrait or picture of any author, composer or artist in connection with his literary, musical or artistic productions which he has sold or disposed of with such name, portrait or picture used in connection therewith.

c. WHAT SHOULD A RELEASE SAY?

Because a release is a legal document, it should contain certain information.

First, it should set out the names and addresses of the parties (that is, the photographer and the subject). Note that the law merely requires the parties' names; it does not require addresses. However, the inclusion of addresses ensures that the parties know how to reach each other.

Second, the release should set out the age of the subject in the photograph. If your subject is a young person, you should ask for identification. This is important because a child (or "minor") may not be legally bound to a signed agreement. If you need to obtain a release from a child you should obtain the name, address, and consent of the child's parent or guardian. Again, in such circumstances you should check to ensure that the person signing is actually the child's parent or guardian. (The age of a child, or a minor, under the law is not the same in all jurisdictions. You may want to check with a lawyer to find out the legal definition of a child in your area.)

The release should also set out the thing of value, or "consideration," that the photographer is giving his or her subject in return for permission to have the photograph used. Such an exchange is not necessary where the contract is "under seal" (that is, where a small red paper wafer, known as a seal, is affixed to the document by the parties' signatures at the time they sign).

The law does not require the consideration given by the photographer to be very valuable. It can be a small amount of money, a copy of the photograph taken by the photographer, or a simple promise to do something such as sending the photograph to a third party.

After setting out the consideration, the release should list the uses that the photographer may make of the picture. The uses may be unlimited, or confined to certain types of use, such as to illustrate an advertisement for a certain type of product. The limitations on use may concern not only the manner or use, but the duration of time during which the picture may be used, or the number of uses which may be made of it. This is the most important part of the release as it defines exactly what the photographer may do with the subject's picture.

The release should also specify *who* may use the photograph. If this isn't specified, the court may interpret the release to mean that only the photographer may use the photograph. Accordingly, if it is possible that the photographer may sell or sign some rights in the photograph to a third party, the release should provide that anyone authorized by the photographer may use it.

A release should specify the photograph in question. If a photographer has taken a number of photographs of a person, a court may hold the release invalid if it cannot determine to which of those photographs the release applies. Accordingly, if more than one photograph of the subject is taken, the release should provide that it applies to any and all photographs of the subject that the photographer has taken.

Finally, the release should provide that it is irrevocable. If this term is not inserted, the release could later be revoked by the person giving it. This term effectively prevents a person from ever retracting the release.

The release should be signed by both parties. It is also helpful to have the signature of the person giving the release witnessed by another person. (Sample #1 shows an example of a release with all these terms.)

d. SHOULD A RELEASE BE IN WRITING?

In states with privacy statutes, such as New York, a release must be in writing to be effective. In Canadian provinces with right to privacy statutes, a release may generally be oral or written, and in some provinces, may be expressed or implied.

In states or provinces without privacy laws, the consent may be oral. However, an oral consent may be difficult to prove, so whenever a release is necessary, it is preferable that it be in writing.

As a practical matter, the parties should execute two copies of the release; one copy should be kept by the photographer, and the other given to the person who is being photographed.

You do not need to give your subject something of value for permission to use a photograph as long as a seal is placed alongside each signature. However, there are cases where a release has been held to be ineffective despite the fact that a

SAMPLE #1
RELEASE

AGREEMENT BETWEEN

JOHN DOE
_____
(name of photographer)
(hereinafter referred to as "the photographer")

- and -

JANET SMITH
_____
(name of model)
(hereinafter referred to as "the model")

In consideration of the payment of ___$100.00_____, the receipt and sufficiency whereof is hereby acknowledged, and the mutual covenants hereinafter set forth, the parties hereto agree as follows:

1. The model hereby consents to and authorizes the use, by the photographer, and the photographer's respective representatives, licensees, successors and assigns, of any and all photographs that the photographer has taken of the model and of the model's property, and of any reproductions of them, for any purpose whatsoever, including, but not by way of limitation, the sale, publication, display, broadcast, and exhibition thereof, in promotion, advertising, trade, and art, whether apart from or in connection with, or illustrative of, any other matter, without any further compensation to the model.

2. The model agrees that the photographs, reproductions, and negatives thereof shall constitute the photographer's sole property, and that the photographer has the full right to dispose of any or all of them in any manner whatsoever.

3. As the photographer proposes to act on this consent forthwith, the model hereby declares it to be irrevocable; and the model hereby releases and discharges the photographer and his respective representatives, licensees, successors and assigns, from all manner of actions, causes of action, debts, accounts, contracts, claims and demands whatsoever which the model or the model's heirs, executors, administrators or assigns can, shall, or may have at any time as a result of any act, matter or thing whatsoever arising out of or in connection with the consent and authorization given by the model in this agreement.

IN WITNESS WHEREOF the parties hereto have executed this agreement.

If model is an adult:

John Doe
_____
(Signature of photographer)

Janet Smith
_____
(Signature of model)

Address and phone number of model or parent/guardian

___111-222 Second Street_____

Anytown, Anywhere

___(666) 999-8888_____

If model is a child
I represent that I am the parent/guardian of the above-named model. I hereby consent to the foregoing on the model's behalf.

_____
(Signature of parent/guardian)

January 1, 199-
_____
(DATE)

seal was affixed to the document, because the parties did not realize the significance of the seal. If is far safer to give your subject something of value. If money is given, it is best to give it by check because then you have a record of the payment. Alternatively, if you agree to send photographs to the subject, send them by registered mail together with a covering letter outlining what they are and why they are being sent to the subject. Again, this gives you some evidence that you have actually met the terms of the release.

e. OBTAINING RELEASES FROM CHILDREN

The law has always considered children to be at a disadvantage when they are signing contracts. They are less experienced, less mature, and less able to resist the pressures and influences of other people. Accordingly, the law generally provides that a contract cannot be enforced against a child.

If you obtain a release from a child, you may not be able to rely on that release as a defense if you are later sued to prevent you from using the photograph.

By common law, a person is considered a child if he or she is under the age of 21 years. Various jurisdictions have reduced this age by statute; Ontario, for example, has reduced the age of majority to 18. To be certain that your release will be binding, you might consider dealing with people under the age of 21 as if they were children, in a legal sense.

The law permits parents or guardians to sign contracts and transact business on a child's behalf. While a child cannot be bound to a contract he or she has signed, the child can be bound if a parent or guardian has signed. Thus, if you wish to obtain a release permitting you to use a child's photograph, the child's parent or guardian should sign it.

Frequently, it is difficult to gauge people's ages. As well, children may tell you that they are older than they actually are. It is no defense to claim a child misrepresented his or her age to you. Courts have concluded in such circumstances that while a child should not be allowed to take advantage of his or her special legal status to support a fraud, and should be forced to compensate a party, the actual contract still cannot be enforced against the child.

Consequently, when photographing young people, it is vitally important to ask for identification if at all practical. If a subject is under 21, it would be wise not to use his or her picture until a release has been signed by a parent or guardian.

f. DEFENSES TO RELEASES

A release, like other legal documents, cannot always specifically provide for every eventuality, and you may have to go to court to determine whether a release applies to a particular situation. There are some common defenses you can use.

1. Ambiguous language

Sometimes the language of the release is vague or open to different interpretations. In such circumstances, a court may rule that the document not be read in favor of the person seeking to enforce it.

In the case of a release, this rule would mean that a court might interpret the document's terms against the photographer. In other words, if a term could be interpreted one way that permits the photographer to use the photograph but also another way that prohibits its use, the court may well choose the interpretation which prevents the photographer from using it.

This rule has been applied with a special rigor in the case of photographic releases. In many situations, the model has often been given one dollar, or some other thing of little value, in return for the right to use his or her picture — a right which may be worth hundreds or even thousands of dollars. The courts have taken the position that it is unfair if a party is forced to give up something of great value for so little in return if that result can reasonably be avoided.

For this reason, it is vitally important to draft photographic releases clearly, and to have them provide as specifically as possible for the uses to which you intend to put the picture.

A good example of the problems caused by a poorly drafted release is the case of Crawford Burton. Burton was a well-known steeplechaser who had signed a release permitting a promotional firm employed by the manufacturer of Camel cigarettes to use his picture in an ad for Camel. Burton was shown in riding clothes, and, by means of an optical illusion, he was depicted in a state of sexual excitement. Burton sued for libel, claiming that this picture exposed him to ridicule. The promotional firm argued that it was entitled to rely on the release signed by Burton, which permitted them to do exactly what they had done, namely, use his picture in an ad for Camel. The court ruled in his favor and noted that his consent to the use of the photographs as an advertisement for which he posed was not a consent to the use of the offending photograph; he had no reason to anticipate that the lens would so distort his appearance.

Unquestionably, a more carefully worded release could have made the promotional argument much more persuasive.

2. "I didn't read it"

The most frequent defense used by people trying to prevent a photographer from using their picture, even though they signed a release, is that they did not read the release and did not know its effect.

The courts used to have a sympathetic ear when someone claimed that he or she did not realize what the document actually said. When education was not as widespread, and legal services were not as available as they are today, the courts took the view that it would be unfair to bind every person to the contract he or she had signed. Some people, such as the infirm or the illiterate, it was thought, should be excused because they just do not have the same intellectual skills as other parties.

Today, however, the courts take a dim view of this argument. The general rule is that when a person signs a document he or she cannot subsequently avoid the obligations incurred under the document simply because he or she did not read it or understand its consequences. The law considers that such people are negligent and therefore should be held to their obligations.

Modern courts have concluded that people are generally on an equal footing, especially with simple agreements. The infirm and the illiterate may still be protected, but these people are fewer than they used to be.

Therefore, if your subject fails to read a release you have prepared, it will still be valid unless your subject is clearly mentally deficient or has some other obvious disability, or you have misled him or her.

Nevertheless, it is safer if you encourage your subjects to read the release, and if you can, have a witness present to attest that you offered such encouragement. That will be of great assistance at a later date. If your subject considers making a claim, the fact that you encouraged the subject to read the release, that someone can verify that you offered some encouragement, and that the subject nevertheless chose not to read it, may discourage a lawsuit. If your subject does take action against you, the fact that you encouraged him or her to read the release, and that he or she did not, will put the subject in a much weaker position in the eyes of the law.

6
COPYRIGHT

a. COPYRIGHT IN THE UNITED STATES

1. Nature and benefits

Many photographers probably view copyright as arcane, complex, and for their purposes, irrelevant. Perhaps that was Abraham Zapruder's opinion, too. As he walked along Elm Street in Dallas one November day in 1963, copyright was probably the farthest thing from his mind. With his 8 mm color movie camera in hand, the Dallas dress manufacturer was looking for a good spot from which to shoot home movies of President Kennedy's visit. He finally decided on a concrete pedestal about four feet high that stood on a slope above the street. From this point, the president's limousine would pass right by him.

When the presidential motorcade came into view, Zapruder started his camera and began photographing the scene. Little did he know the horror his camera would record; just as the car passed by him the President was fatally shot. Zapruder's camera recorded the assassination in vivid detail, capturing such critical aspects as the fatal bullet hitting the President; the shock and fear in the faces of those riding with the President; and the anguish felt by Jacqueline Kennedy when she realized her husband had been shot.

Zapruder's film became one of the most important pieces of evidence in the investigation of the assassination launched by government authorities. It was also a source of considerable profit for Zapruder.

Shortly after the assassination, Zapruder had his film developed and two copies made. Of these three versions, two were given to the secret service, the other, together with all rights in the film, was sold for $150,000 to the publishers of *Time* and *Life* magazines.

The scenes Zapruder recorded made the film important, but copyright made it valuable. Copyright law gave Zapruder the right to contract use of the film; consequently, he had something to sell. The copyright law provided that only people who had Zapruder's permission could use this film, and Zapruder was entitled to charge for giving his permission.

Copyright in the Zapruder film was governed by the Copyright Act of 1909. In 1976, that legislation was replaced by a new act which changed many of the 1909 provisions. Despite these changes, however, the quick thinking of Abraham Zapruder is still relevant to every American photographer, amateur or professional; it illustrates how a knowledge of copyright law can bring profit and prominence.

The Copyright Act of 1976 extends copyright protection to the authors of "original works of authorship" including literary, dramatic, pictorial, graphic, sculptural, artistic, and certain other types of works. Protection is available to both published and unpublished works.

Still photographs are covered under the category of pictorial, graphic, and sculptural work. Movies, video tapes, and slide shows, however, are considered as "audio visual works." They, too, are given copyright protection, but this protection is different in some respects from that given to still photographs. These differences mainly concern —

(a) uses which may be made of the work without the copyright owner's permission, such as in educational and religious contexts, and

(b) cable transmissions which are governed by special rules.

Because these situations are unlikely to be of interest to most photographers, they will not be discussed below.

But not every photograph will be given copyright protection. Court cases have indicated that there are two situations in which a photograph will be denied copyright protection.

First, if a photograph is a blatant copy of another photograph, there is no protection. Second, if a photographer tries to duplicate a photograph by using the same subject, camera angle, lighting, and so on, protection will not be granted.

In one case, a photographer sold the copyright in a nude portrait and then used the same model in a similar pose, for a second portrait. The court held that the second portrait infringed copyright in the first. However, the court reached a different conclusion in a case between the Franklin Mint and National Wildlife Art Exchange. An artist sold copyright in a work, and then copied that work in a second work. The court ruled that the second work did not infringe copyright in the first because the artist copied only the idea from the first work, not its expression.

The best protection against copyright lawsuits is to introduce as many variations as are artistically feasible in a photograph. In a few instances, though, even this approach may not save a photographer from being successfully sued for infringement of copyright.

The owner of copyright in a photograph has the exclusive right to —

(a) reproduce the copyright work in copies;

(b) prepare derivative works based on the copyright work;

(c) distribute copies of the copyright work to the public by sale or other transfer of ownership, or by rental, lease, or loan;

(d) perform the copyright work publicly, in the case of motion pictures and other audio-visual works;

(e) display the copyright work publicly, in the case of still photographs, including the individual images of a motion picture or other audio-visual works; and

(f) authorize anyone else to act on these rights.

The second exclusive right, that of preparing a derivative work, is especially important. It means that no one may copy a copyright work in a different medium. Thus, copyright in a photograph will preclude unauthorized copying by drawing, or in any other form, as well as by photographic reproduction. This principle was recently reaffirmed in a case which concerned the Zapruder films discussed earlier. In the case of *Time, Inc. vs. Bernard Geis Associates*, certain frames of the Zapruder film, which Zapruder sold to Time, were copied in charcoal sketches in a book on the Kennedy assassination without Time's permission. The court held that these sketches would constitute an infringement of the copyright in the Zapruder film, except for the nature of the subject matter and the context of the defendant's reproduction which rendered it a fair use. Fair use is discussed under item **9.** in this section.

In general, it is illegal for anyone to violate any of the rights provided to the owner of copyright. However, these rights are subject to certain limitations. The limitations are set out in the act, and are basically exemptions from liability for infringement of copyright in certain situations. The most important of these situations are instances of fair use.

It is important to remember that copyright protection extends only to a photograph, negative, slide, or motion picture itself; it does not extend to the idea, concept, location, or thing depicted in the photograph.

For example, it would be an infringement of copyright for you to copy a photograph of the New York skyline without the copyright owner's permission; but it would not be an infringement for you to go to the same location, and under the same conditions, take a photograph. You are free to copy the original; you are not free to copy the copy.

The Copyright Act also extends copyright protection to paintings, sculpture, drawings, cartoons, posters, toys, statues, maps, record jackets, diagrams, architectural drawings, and advertisements.

2. Acquisition

Copyright exists in a work from the time the work is created. Generally, the copyright immediately becomes the property of the author who created the work. Only the author or those deriving their rights through the author can claim copyright.

However, there is an important exception to the general rule. When a work is "made for hire," the employer, not the employee, is considered the author. A work is made for hire when it is prepared by an employee within the scope of his or her employment; or when the parties agree in writing that a work shall be considered a work made for hire.

The nationality of the person creating the work is important in determining when, if at all, a work should be given copyright protection. The nationality of the person creating the work has a different effect on copyright protection depending on whether the work he or she has created is unpublished or published.

If a photograph is unpublished, it will be given copyright protection in the United States, regardless of where the author lives or his or her citizenship. If, however, copies of the work have been published, the work will only be given copyright protection in the United States if —

(a) on the date of its first publication, the author is a citizen, or living in the United States, or is a citizen, or living in some other country that has a copyright treaty with the United States; or

(b) copies of the work are first published in the United States, or in some other country that, on the date of publication, is either a party to the Universal Copyright Convention, or is the subject of a presidential proclamation.

The copyright office publishes a helpful circular, *International Copyright Relations of the United States*. It lists the copyright relations the United States has with dozens of other countries, and specifies the treaties those countries have signed with the United States, if any, whether those countries have signed the Universal Copyright Convention, and whether they are subject of a presidential proclamation.

No publication or registration of the copyright office is necessary to secure copyright under the act; copyright is secured automatically when the work is created. However, copyright may be lost if, when copies of the work are first distributed to the public, all copies distributed do not bear a notice of copyright, or the work has not been registered before, or within five years after copies are first distributed to the public and a reasonable effort has not been made to correct the omission.

3.   Copyright notice

When copies of a work are first distributed to the public, a notice of copyright should be placed on all publicly distributed copies. This notice is required even on work published outside the United States. Failure to place the notice can result in the loss of certain additional rights otherwise available to the copyright owner. The use of the copyright notice is the responsibility of the copyright owner and does not require advance permission from or registration with the copyright office.

The copyright notice should contain all of the following three elements:

(a) The letter "c" in a circle printed as © or the word "copyright" or the abbreviation "copr."

(b) The year of the first publication of the work

(c) The name of the owner of copyright and the work, or an abbreviation by which the name can be recognized, or a generally known alternative designation of the owner

The copyright notice should be put on the material in a noticeable position. The Registrar of Copyright has provided that where a work is reproduced in two-dimensional copies, as is a photograph, "a notice affixed directly or by means of a label cemented, sewn, or otherwise attached durably, so as to withstand normal use of the front or back of the copies, or to any backing, mounting, matting, framing, or other material to which the copies are durably attached, so as to withstand normal use, or in which they are permanently housed, is acceptable."

The omission of the copyright notice can have a serious impact. Where the notice has been omitted, copyright in a work is valid only if —

(a) the notice has been omitted from only a few copies distributed to the public;

(b) copyright registration was made before the publication without notice, or is made within five years after, and a reasonable effort is made to add this notice to all copies distributed to the public in the U.S. after the omission has been discovered; or

(c) the copyright owner required a third party in writing to put the copyright notice on works distributed to the public, but that third party failed to do so.

While copyright is not invalidated where a notice has been omitted in these circumstances, anyone who was led to believe by that omission that there was no copyright in the work is not liable for damages for infringement they commit before actually being informed that the copyright claim on the work has been registered.

Occasionally, people will put a copyright notice on their work but will make an error in the name or the date or even omit entirely either the name or the date. If the name is incorrect or omitted, the validity and ownership of the copyright are not affected. In such a case, however, any person who innocently does something that infringes the copyright has a complete defense if they can prove they were misled by the notice and began the activity in good faith.

If the year given in a copyright notice is earlier than the year in which publication first occurred, the copyright period is deemed to start running from the year given in the notice. Where the year given in the notice is more than one year later than the year in which publication first occurred, however, the work is considered to have been published without any notice at all.

4. Deposit and registration

Within three months after a work has been published with notice of copyright in the United States, the owner of copyright or of the exclusive right of publication in that work must deposit two copies of the work in the copyright office. Where the work is first published in a foreign country, two copies of it must be deposited in the copyright office as soon as the work is published in the United States (that is, as soon as copies are distributed to the public either as imports or as part of an American edition).

The deposit requirement ensures that the Library of Congress receives copies of every copyright work published or distributed in the United States for its collections, or for use in national library programs. The act essentially provides that deposit of a work is voluntary. However, it also provides that the Registrar of Copyright may make a written demand for the deposit of a work at any time after publication. If the deposit is not made within three months of this demand, you may be fined. However, failure to deposit copies as required does not invalidate the copyright.

The copyright office has specified that the deposit requirements for photographs are as follows:

(a) Size and finish in descending order of preference

   (i) the most widely distributed edition

   (ii) 8 x 10-inch glossy print

   (iii) other size or finish

(b) Unmounted rather than mounted

(c) Archival quality rather than less permanent paper stock or printing process

If the work has been published with a copyright notice, copies sent to the copyright office should also show the copyright notice, including its content and position on the work.

The act does not require copies of *unpublished* works to be deposited with the copyright office. However, if you do register an unpublished photograph with the copyright office you must deposit one copy of it.

Further information about registration and deposit can be obtained from the copyright office by writing for *Simultaneous Deposit of the Elements for Registration*.

Copyright registration is ordinarily voluntary; it is not required to secure copyright protection under the present law. But registration allows copyright owners a broader range of remedies in infringement suits. Moreover, some people buying photographs are comforted if they are shown a copy of a registration certificate. Accordingly, registration is often advisable if a work is likely to become important to the photographer, either because of possible lawsuits or because the work may be copied and sold.

There is one exception to the general rule that copyright registration is not required. Registration may be required to preserve a copyright that would otherwise be invalidated because of the omission of a copyright notice from the published copies, or omission of the name or date, or an error in the date in the notice.

To register a claim to copyright in a work, you should send the following three elements in the same envelope or package to the Registrar of Copyright:

(a) A properly completed application form. (A sample copy of the application is shown in Sample #2.)

(b) A non-refundable fee of $10, payable to the "Registrar of Copyright."

(c) A deposit of the work being registered.

When applying for registration, use only the officially printed application form (in the case of photographs, this is Form VA— see Sample #3). Photocopies or other reproductions of the application form will not be accepted by the Registrar of Copyright. The copyright office has a special "copyright hotline" (202-287-9100) which you may phone at any time to order copyright registration application forms. Thses forms are supplied free of charge. Alternatively, you may request forms by writing —

Information and Publications Section
LN-455, Copyright Office
Library of Congress
Washington, D.C 20559

SAMPLE #2
APPLICATION FOR COPYRIGHT
REGISTRATION(U.S.)

FORM VA
UNITED STATES COPYRIGHT OFFICE

REGISTRATION NUMBER

VA	VAU

EFFECTIVE DATE OF REGISTRATION

Month	Day	Year

DO NOT WRITE ABOVE THIS LINE. IF YOU NEED MORE SPACE, USE A SEPARATE CONTINUATION SHEET.

1

TITLE OF THIS WORK ▼

RAINFOREST

NATURE OF THIS WORK ▼ See instructions

PHOTOGRAPH

PREVIOUS OR ALTERNATIVE TITLES ▼

N/A

PUBLICATION AS A CONTRIBUTION If this work was published as a contribution to a periodical, serial, or collection, give information about the collective work in which the contribution appeared.   **Title of Collective Work ▼**

If published in a periodical or serial give: **Volume ▼**   **Number ▼**   **Issue Date ▼**   **On Pages ▼**

2

a

NAME OF AUTHOR ▼

JOHN DOE

DATES OF BIRTH AND DEATH
Year Born ▼   Year Died ▼
1950

Was this contribution to the work a "work made for hire"?
☐ Yes
☒ No

AUTHOR'S NATIONALITY OR DOMICILE
Name of Country
OR { Citizen of ▶ United States
Domiciled in ▶ United States

WAS THIS AUTHOR'S CONTRIBUTION TO THE WORK
Anonymous?   ☐ Yes ☒ No
Pseudonymous?   ☐ Yes ☒ No
If the answer to either of these questions is "Yes," see detailed instructions

NATURE OF AUTHORSHIP Briefly describe nature of the material created by this author in which copyright is claimed. ▼
PHOTOGRAPH

NOTE

Under the law, the "author" of a work made for hire is generally the employer, not the employee (see instructions). For any part of this work that was made for hire check "Yes" in the space provided, give the employer (or other person for whom the work was prepared) as "Author" of that part, and leave the space for dates of birth and death blank.

b

NAME OF AUTHOR ▼

DATES OF BIRTH AND DEATH
Year Born ▼   Year Died ▼

Was this contribution to the work a "work made for hire"?
☐ Yes
☐ No

AUTHOR'S NATIONALITY OR DOMICILE
Name of Country
OR { Citizen of ▶
Domiciled in ▶

WAS THIS AUTHOR'S CONTRIBUTION TO THE WORK
Anonymous?   ☐ Yes ☐ No
Pseudonymous?   ☐ Yes ☐ No
If the answer to either of these questions is "Yes," see detailed instructions

NATURE OF AUTHORSHIP Briefly describe nature of the material created by this author in which copyright is claimed. ▼

c

NAME OF AUTHOR ▼

DATES OF BIRTH AND DEATH
Year Born ▼   Year Died ▼

Was this contribution to the work a "work made for hire"?
☐ Yes
☐ No

AUTHOR'S NATIONALITY OR DOMICILE
Name of Country
OR { Citizen of ▶
Domiciled in ▶

WAS THIS AUTHOR'S CONTRIBUTION TO THE WORK
Anonymous?   ☐ Yes ☐ No
Pseudonymous?   ☐ Yes ☐ No
If the answer to either of these questions is "Yes," see detailed instructions

NATURE OF AUTHORSHIP Briefly describe nature of the material created by this author in which copyright is claimed. ▼

3

YEAR IN WHICH CREATION OF THIS WORK WAS COMPLETED This information must be given in all cases.
1986 ◀ Year

DATE AND NATION OF FIRST PUBLICATION OF THIS PARTICULAR WORK
Complete this information ONLY if this work has been published.
Month ▶ January   Day ▶ 01   Year ▶ 199-
◀ Nation

4

COPYRIGHT CLAIMANT(S) Name and address must be given even if the claimant is the same as the author given in space 2. ▼
John Smith
123 - 1st Street
Anytown, Anystate 12345

See instructions before completing this space

TRANSFER If the claimant(s) named here in space 4 are different from the author(s) named in space 2, give a brief statement of how the claimant(s) obtained ownership of the copyright. ▼

APPLICATION RECEIVED

ONE DEPOSIT RECEIVED

TWO DEPOSITS RECEIVED

REMITTANCE NUMBER AND DATE

DO NOT WRITE HERE OFFICE USE ONLY

MORE ON BACK ▶   • Complete all applicable spaces (numbers 5-9) on the reverse side of this page
• See detailed instructions   • Sign the form at line 8

DO NOT WRITE HERE
Page 1 of _____ pages

SAMPLE #2 — Continued

EXAMINED BY	FORM VA
CHECKED BY	
☐ CORRESPONDENCE Yes	FOR COPYRIGHT OFFICE USE ONLY
☐ DEPOSIT ACCOUNT FUNDS USED	

DO NOT WRITE ABOVE THIS LINE. IF YOU NEED MORE SPACE, USE A SEPARATE CONTINUATION SHEET.

PREVIOUS REGISTRATION Has registration for this work, or for an earlier version of this work, already been made in the Copyright Office?
☐ Yes ☒ No If your answer is "Yes," why is another registration being sought? (Check appropriate box) ▼
☐ This is the first published edition of a work previously registered in unpublished form.
☐ This is the first application submitted by this author as copyright claimant.
☐ This is a changed version of the work, as shown by space 6 on this application.
If your answer is "Yes," give **Previous Registration Number ▼**   **Year of Registration ▼**

5

DERIVATIVE WORK OR COMPILATION Complete both space 6a & 6b for a derivative work, complete only 6b for a compilation.
a. **Preexisting Material** Identify any preexisting work or works that this work is based on or incorporates. ▼

N/A

b. **Material Added to This Work** Give a brief, general statement of the material that has been added to this work and in which copyright is claimed. ▼

N/A

6

See instructions before completing this space

DEPOSIT ACCOUNT If the registration fee is to be charged to a Deposit Account established in the Copyright Office, give name and number of Account
Name ▼   **Account Number ▼**

N/A

7

CORRESPONDENCE Give name and address to which correspondence about this application should be sent. Name/Address/Apt/City/State/Zip ▼

John Smith
123 - 1st Street
Anytown, Anystate 12345

Area Code & Telephone Number ▶

Be sure to give your daytime phone number

CERTIFICATION* I, the undersigned, hereby certify that I am the
Check only one ▼
☒ author
☐ other copyright claimant
☐ owner of exclusive right(s)
☐ authorized agent of _____
Name of author or other copyright claimant or owner of exclusive right(s) ▲

of the work identified in this application and that the statements made
by me in this application are correct to the best of my knowledge.

Typed or printed name and date ▼ If this is a published work, this date must be the same as or later than the date of publication given in space 3.
John Smith
date ▶ January 4, 199-

Handwritten signature (X) ▼   John Smith

8

MAIL CERTIFICATE TO

Certificate will be mailed in window envelope

Name ▼
John Smith
Number/Street/Apartment Number ▼
123 - 1st Street
City/State/Zip ▼
Anytown, Anystate 12345

Have you:
• Completed all necessary spaces?
• Signed your application in space 8?
• Enclosed check or money order for $10 payable to Register of Copyrights?
• Enclosed your deposit material with the application and fee?
MAIL TO: Register of Copyrights Library of Congress Washington DC 20559

9

* 17 U.S.C. § 506(e): Any person who knowingly makes a false representation of a material fact in the application for copyright registration provided for by section 409, or in any written statement filed in connection with the application, shall be fined not more than $2,500.

U.S. GOVERNMENT PRINTING OFFICE: 1984—421-278/514

May 1984—30,000

A copyright registration is effective on the date the copyright office receives the required elements in acceptable form, regardless of the length of time it takes to process the application and mail the certificate of registration.

Applications should be sent to —

Registrar of Copyright
Library of Congress
Washington, D.C. 20559

Filling out application Form VA is an art in itself, so it's important to follow the guidelines below.

(a) Part 1, Title

In order for your work to be identified, you must give it a title. Indexing, other registration, and future identification of the work will depend on the information you give here. If your work is being registered as a contribution to a periodical, serial, or collection, give the title of the contribution in the "Title of This Work" space. Then, in the line headed "Publication as a Contribution," give information about the collective work in which the contribution appeared. Under the heading "Nature of This Work" briefly describe the general nature or character of the pictorial, graphic, or sculptural work being registered for copyright, e.g. — "photograph."

(b) Part 2, Author

Unless the work was "made for hire," the individual who actually created the work is its "author." In the case of work made for hire, the act provides that "the employer or other person for whom the work was prepared is considered the author." As noted above, a work made for hire is defined as

i. a work prepared by an employee within the scope of his or her employment; or

ii. a work specially ordered or commissioned for use as a contribution to a collective work, as part of a motion picture or other audio visual work... as a supplementary work, as a compilation, as an instructional text,...if the parties expressly

133

agree in a written instrument signed by them that the work shall be considered a "work made for hire."

Under "Name of Author" give the fullest form of the author's name. If you have checked "yes" to indicate that the work was made for hire, you must give the full legal name of the employer or other person for whom the work was prepared. Under dates of birth and death, the author's birth date is optional, but it is useful as a form of identification. Leave this space blank if the author's contribution was a "work made for hire." Under "Author's Nationality or Domicile" give the country of which the author is a citizen or the country in which the author lives. Nationality or domicile must be given in all cases. Under "Nature of Authorship" give a brief, general statement of the nature of this particular author's contribution to the work. In the case of a photograph, merely put "photograph."

(c) Part 3, Creation and publication

Do not confuse creation with publication. Every application for copyright registration must state the year in which creation of the work was completed. Give the date and nation of first publication only if the work has been published.

Under "Creation" a work is created when it is fixed in a copy for the first time. The date you give here should be the year in which the author completed the particular version for which registration is now being sought, even if other versions exist or if further changes or additions are planned.

Under the heading "Publication," remember that publication is defined in the act as "the distribution of copies…of a work to the public by sale or other transfer of ownership, or by rental, lease, or lending." Give the full date when, and the country where, publication first occurred. If first publication took place simultaneously in the United States and other countries, it is sufficient to state "U.S.A."

(d) Part 4, Claimant

Give the name and address of the copyright claimant in this work even if the claimant is also the author. If the copyright claimant is not the author, the application for registration must contain "a brief statement of how the claimant obtained ownership of the copyright." If any copyright claimant named in Part 4 is not an author named in Part 2, give a brief, general statement summarizing the means by which that claimant obtained ownership of the copyright. For example, one can put "by written contract," "by transfer of all rights from the author," "assignment," or "by will." Do not attach transferred documents.

(e) Part 8, Certification

The application will not be accepted by the Copyright Office unless it bears the date and the handwritten signature of the author or other copyright claimant, or the owner of exclusive rights, or the duly authorized agent of the author, claimant, or owner of exclusive rights. If you check the box before "Author" it means that you, the individual, are the person named in Part 2 of the application. Do not check this box if you are not a person named in Part 2.

If you check the box before "Other Copyright Claimant" it means that you, the individual, are not the author of the work as named in Part 2, but that you have obtained ownership of all the rights under the copyright initially belonging to the author. In this event, you will have named the actual author in Part 2, and will have completed Part 4 with your name and address as well as an explanation of how the copyright was transferred from the author to you. If you check the box before "Owner of Exclusive Rights" it means that, while you, as an individual, are neither the author nor the copyright claimant, you are the owner even if only for a limited time or geographical area, of one or more of the exclusive rights which constitute the full copyright. Again,

135

Part 2 will contain the name of the author and Part 4 will contain the name and address of the copyright claimant.

Finally, if you check the box before "Authorized Agent of" it means that you are not signing for yourself as an individual, but as the authorized representative either of the author or other copyright claimant or of the owner of exclusive rights. When you check this box, you will also give, on the dotted line which follows it, the name of the person or entity on whose behalf you are signing the application.

5. Ownership

Generally, the photographer owns the copyright in his or her work. An exception is a work made for hire, where the employer or other person for whom the work was prepared owns the copyright unless the parties have expressly agreed otherwise in a written agreement.

"A work made for hire" is defined in section 101 as

1. a work prepared by an employee within the scope of his or her employment;

2. a work specially ordered or commissioned for use as a contribution to a collective work, as part of a motion picture or other audio visual work,...as a supplementary work, as a compilation, as an instructional text,...or as an atlas, if the parties expressly agree in a written instrument signed by them that the work shall be considered a work made for hire.

A "supplementary work" is defined as a work prepared for publication as a secondary adjunct to a work by another author for the purpose of introducing, concluding, illustrating, explaining, revising, commenting upon, or assisting in the use of the other work, such as a pictorial illustration.

The question of ownership is easy to resolve when a photographer is on the full-time staff of an organization like a newspaper; in these circumstances, copyright and the pictures the photographer creates are undoubtedly owned by the employer. Similarly, it is equally clear that copyright is not owned by the photographer who actually takes the picture where that picture is specially ordered or commissioned for use as a contribution to an encyclopedia, anthology, or movie, when the parties have agreed in writing that the picture will not be owned by the photographer.

Apart from these two situations, however, there are a range of instances where there has been debate about who owns copyright in a picture. Photographers selling freelance work, photographers who take portraits of other people on request, and photographers who are engaged to take pictures of some thing or event all fall into an ambiguous area of the law.

The Copyright Act appears to draw the line in these situations in favor of the photographer, unless the photographer was an employee, or unless the photographer was taking a picture for inclusion in a certain kind of work, and it was agreed in writing that the photographer should not have copyright in the work.

Photographers should also understand that ownership of a photograph, manuscript, painting, or any other copy of a thing does not give the possessor copyright in it. In practice, this is both good and bad news for photographers. It is bad news in the sense that if you own a painting, the fact that you own it does not convey any of the rights of copyright in it. In other words, the fact that you own it does not mean that you can do with it all the things that a copyright owner can do with his work. For example, you could not photograph this painting and sell copies of that photograph. Only the creator of the work, in this case the painter, could do that.

The good news is that if you take a picture and sell someone a copy of it, that person cannot, in turn, reprint your picture and sell it without your permission. He or she does not have copyright in the photograph even though he or she owns a print of it.

6. Duration

Copyright in a photograph created on or after January 1, 1978 endures for the life of the author, and 50 years after the author's death.

There are, however, certain exceptions to this general rule. First, in the case of an anonymous work (that is, no natural person is identified as the author on copies of the work), a pseudonymous work (that is, the author is identified under a fictitious name on copies of the work), or work made for hire, the copyright endures for a term of 75 years from the year of its first publication, or a term of 100 years from the year of its creation, whichever expires first.

Second, there are special provisions for works created before January 1, 1978. These requirements are complicated and will be summarized briefly here. If you wish more detailed information you should consult sections 303 and 304 of the act.

Copyright in a work created before January 1, 1978, but not at that time in the public domain or copyright, exists from January 1, 1978, and endures for the life of the author 50 years after the author's death, except if it is anonymous work, pseudonymous work, or a work made for hire (see above). In no case, however, shall the term of copyright in such a work expire before December 31, 2002; and if the work is published before December 31, 2002, the term of copyright shall not expire before December 31, 2027.

7. Assignments and licenses

Any or all of the exclusive rights of the copyright owner may be transferred. These rights consist of the right to reproduce the copyright work in copies; the right to prepare derivative works based upon the copyright work; the right to distribute copies of the work to the public by sale or other transfer of ownership, or by rental, lease, or loan; and, in the case of pictorial, graphic, or sculptural works, including the individual images of a motion picture or other audio-visual work, to display publicly the copyright at work.

A transfer of the copyright owner's rights may be limited by time, use, or geographical location, as the copyright owner chooses. Thus, you may allow another party to use a photograph you have taken for a specific period of time, such as a year; or in a specific way, such as for an illustration in a certain magazine, for a story on a certain topic, or an advertisement for a certain product; or in a specific area, such as your home town, a state, or the continental United States.

There are certain legal requirements regarding transfers. The most important is the need for a written record of the transfer. The law provides that every transfer of exclusive rights must be in writing and signed by the owner or the owner's agent, to be valid. Transfer of a right on a nonexclusive basis does not need to be in writing, but it is still a good idea, as both parties then have a written record of the actual terms of their agreement.

Second, there may be state laws and regulations that govern the ownership or transfer of personal property, the requirements for valid contracts, or the proper conduct of business. These laws and regulations may well apply to transfer of copyright. If you are considering making a transfer, it would be wise to consult with an attorney in your state about any laws or regulations that might apply to you.

Third, the act does not require transfers to be recorded in the copyright office, but there are certain legal advantages to doing so. For example, the Copyright Act provides that recording a transfer gives notice to all persons of the transfer if —

(a) the transfer specifically identifies the work so that the transfer would be revealed by a reasonable search under the work's title or regulation number in copyright office records; and

(b) the work has been registered in the copyright office.

Accordingly, if you decide to have your transfer recorded, make sure you obtain registration of a copyright claim in the work as well, and identify the work in the transfer by the title or registration number given to it when it is registered.

As well, the act provides that no legal action for infringement of copyright can be instituted by a person who holds copyright by way of transfer unless the transfer has been recorded in the copyright office.

Finally, when a person transfers some exclusive right, the recording of the transfer will effectively prevent that person from transferring those same rights again to another person.

The owner of any particular exclusive right is entitled to all the protection and remedies given to the copyright owner. For example, if a person has received by transfer the right to make copies of a work in the continental United States, and someone else makes copies without permission, the owner may sue for copyright infringement.

For information about recording copyright transfers, write to Circular R12 from —

The Information and Publications Section
LN-455, Copyright Office
Library of Congress
Washington, D.C. 20559

If you are making a transfer of copyright, these elements should be written in your transfer document:

(a) The date your transfer agreement is made

(b) The full name and address of each party

(c) The work in question, identified by its title or copyright registration number, or both

(d) The rights being transferred and any limitations, such as the time period during which the transfer is effective, the type of use the party receiving the transfer is entitled to make of the work, or the geographic area in which the party receiving the transfer is able to exercise the rights given

(e) The date the transfer begins if it is different from the date the agreement is made

(f) The money or other consideration being paid

(g) A statement that you are the owner of copyright in the work and are entitled to make the transfer

(h) The ages of the parties if there is any doubt that either is below the age of majority (at the same time ask for proof of age)

(See Sample #3 for an example of an assignment of copyright.)

8. Infringement

The owner of copyright has the exclusive right to do and authorize certain things, such as reproduce the copyright work, prepare derivative works, and distribute copies to the public. Subject to one exception (see section 9 on "fair use") anyone who does any of these things without the copyright owner's permission infringes the owner's copyright.

Most cases of infringement are easily identified. Someone may reproduce a photograph you have taken and sell copies of it to the public without your permission. Or someone may buy, or recopy, a photograph you have taken and sell it to a magazine or newspaper as his or her own work.

Some cases of infringement may be more difficult to spot, and photographers should be on the lookout for them. An often overlooked area of infringement involves "derivative" works, or works that exist in a form different from that of the original. For example, it would be infringement of copyright

141

SAMPLE #3
ASSIGNMENT OF COPYRIGHT (U.S.)

old p. 138 199-

AGREEMENT made this 1st **day of** February _____ , 199-__

BETWEEN:

_____ John Doe _____
(name of transferor)
(hereinafter referred to as "the transferor")

- and -

_____ Jim Smith _____
(name of transferee)
(hereinafter referred to as "the transferee")

IN CONSIDERATION of the payment of ___ $100.00 ___ , the sufficiency
and receipt whereof is hereby acknowledged, the transferor, being the owner
of copyright in a photograph entitled ___ "Rainforest" ___ , registered
with the United States Copyright Office on ___ January 4, 199- ___ ,
and bearing the registration number 1-111-111 , hereby agrees to transfer
all right, title, and interest (including the right to secure copyright therein) in
the said photograph to the transferee.

IN WITNESS WHEREOF the parties hereto have executed this Agreement.

_____ *John Doe* _____
Transferor

_____ *Jim Smith* _____
Transferee

142

in a photograph to make a sketch of the scene or people depicted in that photograph. (Note, however, it is only infringement if the person sketches from the photograph; it would not be infringement for the person to go to the same spot, or to the same person and make the sketch independently.) Moreover, because the transfer of ownership of any material object does not convey any rights in a copyright work embodied in the object, it may well be infringement for someone who buys a photograph form you to make that photograph into a poster and sell copies of it to the public.

If you are the owner of copyright in a work and you believe that copyright has been infringed upon, you may institute an action for infringement. If you win your action, the act provides for a number of remedies. These remedies include the destruction or other reasonable disposition of all copies made or used in violation of your copyright and payment of damages. Damages can be actual damages and any additional profits the infringing party made, or if you choose before final judgment is rendered, "statutory damages" (a sum of not less than $250 or more than $10,000, whichever the court considers just.) Statutory damages are especially useful where a copyright owner may not have suffered any damage, or will have a difficult time proving loss.

Any person who infringes copyright willfully and for the purpose of commercial advantage or private financial gain may be guilty of criminal infringement and, if convicted, may be fined not more than $10,000 or imprisoned for not more than a year, or both.

While the act ensures that copyright owners can protect their copyright and derive full benefit from it, it also ensures that people who legitimately obtain copies of a work from a copyright owner can use them in a reasonable manner. For example, the owner of a copy of a work that has been lawfully made is entitled, without having to obtain permission from the copyright owner, to sell or otherwise dispose of that copy. Moreover, the owner of a copy of a work lawfully made is entitled to display that copy publicly. These privileges, however, do not extend to any person who has acquired possession of the copy from a copyright owner by rental, lease, loan, or otherwise, without acquiring ownership of it.

Finally, if you own copyright in a photograph that portrays a useful article (such as an automobile), you cannot prevent someone from making a copy of your photograph where the car is shown unless you also have rights in the car itself. Further, copyright in a useful article (such as a car) that has been offered for sale or other distribution to the public is not infringed by someone making, distributing, or displaying a photograph of it in connection with a news report, advertisement, or commentary relating to its distribution or display. Thus, the owner of the copyright in a car could not sue you if you took a photograph of the car and distributed copies of it in connection with a news article on the car or for the purpose of selling the car.

9. Fair use

It is not considered infringement of copyright to make "fair use" of a work. Fair use is not defined in the act. Indeed, U.S. courts have been unable to come up with a single definition of it since the concept came into being.

The courts have, however, evolved a set of criteria which provides some gauge for determining whether copyright exists in a particular case. These criteria have now been summarized and embodied in section 107 of the act:

> Notwithstanding the provisions of section 106, the fair use of a copyright work, including such used by reproduction in copies...or by any other means specified by that section for purposes such as criticism, comments, news, reporting, teaching (including multiple copies for classroom use), scholarship, or research, is not an infringement of copyright. In determining whether the

use made of work in any particular case is a fair use, the factors to be considered shall include:

i. the purpose and character of the use, including whether such use is of a commercial nature or is for nonprofit educational purposes;

ii. the nature of the copyright work;

iii. the amount and substantiality of the portion used in relation to the copyright work as a whole; and

iv. the effect of the use upon the potential market for or value of the copyright work.

As this section indicates, whether the use of a work without permission of the copyright owner is to be considered fair will depend on the purpose of the use, the nature of the work, the amount of the work used, and the effect of the use on the market for or value of the work.

The vast majority of cases on fair use do not concern photographs. Rather, they concern books or articles that have been quoted to a great extent, or even printed in their entirety, by someone without the copyright owner's permission. However, the cases concerning photographs are sufficient to conclude that the most important factor in the eyes of a court in determining whether an unauthorized use of copyright work is fair is the effect of the use on a potential market for or value of the copyright work. If one person makes use of another's work so that the value of the original is diminished, that will not be considered to be fair use. If, however, there is no market for the work, or the copyright owner never intended to sell copies of it, a court might consider an unauthorized use to be fair.

A recent illustration of the application of this principle of fair use concerns the Zapruder films of Kennedy's assassination, discussed earlier. Time, Inc. had purchased copyright in the film and parts of it were printed in several issues of *Life* magazine.

145

Later, Bernard Geis Associates published the book *Six Seconds in Dallas,* a study of the assassination. While writing the book, the author attempted to persuade Time, Inc. to permit him to use copies of portions of the Zapruder film. He was unsuccessful. But because the Zapruder film was important to the theory advanced in his book, the author nevertheless decided to use it. Perhaps concerned about the possibility of an action for copyright infringement, he did not reproduce the Zapruder film photographically, but employed an artist to make copies in charcoal by means of a sketch.

When Time, Inc. discovered that portions of the Zapruder film had been included in the book, it sued for copyright infringement. In defense, the defendants alleged that they had made fair use of the film.

The court ruled in favor of the defendants. In making its decision, it stated that there was a public interest in having the fullest information available on the murder of President Kennedy. Also, the court found that there had been no injury to Time, Inc. and because no competition existed between the two parties the value of the photographs was not affected.

If you are considering using another's photograph without permission, note the wording of the act and consider whether your use could come within the factors set out there. It would also be wise to consult an attorney for a legal opinion on the question.

10.   More information

The copyright office has spent considerable effort in disseminating information on copyright law. In particular, it has published, and will distribute at no charge, pamphlets on various aspects of copyright law. These pamphlets, known as circulars, can be obtained by writing to —

Information and Publications Section
LN-455, Copyright Office
Library of Congress
Washington, D.C. 20559

Please note that the copyright office is not permitted to give legal advice. In particular, it will not comment upon the merits, copyright status, or ownership of particular works, or upon the extent of protection afforded to particular works by copyright law. Nor will it advise on questions of possible copyright infringement or prosecution of copyright violations, or draft or interpret contract terms. All of these services should be provided by an attorney.

In addition to offering general information on copyright law, the copyright office provides for a fee copies of copyright office records and deposits. These records and deposits can help you determine whether someone holds copyright in a particular work, and who that person or entity is.

You may request copies of copyright office records either in person or in writing. If you request them in writing, your request should —

(a) clearly identify the type of records you wish to obtain,

(b) specify whether you require certified or uncertified copies (certified copies cost more, and are only required for litigation),

(c) clearly identify the specific record to be copied. Your request should include the following specific information if possible:

    (i)   The type of work involved (for example, photograph)

   (ii)   The registration number of the work

  (iii)   The year of registration

  (iv)   The complete title of the work

   (v)   The author, including any pseudonym by which the author may be known

  (vi)   The claimants

 (vii)   If the requested copy is of an assignment, license, contract, or other recorded document, the volume and page number of the recorded document

(d) include the fee, and

(e) include your telephone number and address so that the copyright office may contact you

If the year of the registration and the title of the work are not provided, a search of the copyright office records may be required for purposes of verification; there is an hourly fee for this service.

The copyright office will provide reproductions of works deposited in connection with the copyright registration and held in its custody only if the copyright author gives the copyright office written authorization, or the request is from an attorney on behalf of a party involved in copyright litigation, or from a court hearing a court case concerning copyright.

For information about doing research in the records of the copyright office, write for Circular R22, *How to Investigate the Copyright Status of a Work*, or write to —

Reference and Bibliography Section
LN-450, Copyright Office
Library of Congress
Washington, D.C. 20559

b. COPYRIGHT IN CANADA

When the actress Farrah Fawcett was at the height of her fame, millions of people around the world watched her on TV and in movies and bought posters with her photograph. One of her posters became a best selling poster, with over four million copies sold.

A Canadian poster manufacturer, Campus Crafts Holdings Ltd., obtained a copy of the popular poster, had it photographed and produced copies, all without the copyright owner's permission. Approximately 140,000 of these counter-feit copies were made and sold across Canada.

Eventually the scheme was discovered by the copyright owner, an Ohio company known as Pro Arts Inc., who promptly sued Campus Crafts for copyright infringement. In due course, Pro Arts received damages from Campus Crafts totalling almost $300,000.

This case demonstrates how important a tool copyright can be for a photographer. It ensures that photographers receive the fruit of their labor, and are able to prevent others from wrongfully using them. Accordingly, it is useful for every photographer to have an understanding of copyright and its benefits.

1. Nature and benefits

The Copyright Act defines copyright as —

> the sole right to produce or reproduce a work or any substan-tial part thereof in any material form whatever. It applies to every original literary, dramatic, musical and artistic work, including photographs.

The Copyright Act extends copyright protection to the creators of works where, at the time the work was made, the author was at least one of the following:

(a) A Canadian citizen, British subject, or both

(b) A resident within Her Majesty's dominions

(c) A citizen or subject of a country belonging to the Berne Copyright Convention

(d) A citizen or subject of a country belonging to the Universal Copyright Convention or which grants by treaty, convention, agreement, or law to citizens of Canada the benefits of its copyright statute on sub-stantially the same basis as to its own citizens

If an author meets these requirements, he or she can acquire copyright protection merely by creating an original work. Copyright comes into being as soon as the work is made; no registration or placement of a notice is required for the work to be given copyright protection in this country.

The work must be *created* and *original* to be entitled to copyright. For photographers, this means there must be a negative, or a print, for their work to be protected as a creation. On the other hand, to meet the originality requirement, the work must not be copied from another work. It does not have to be artistic, or creative — just original. All photographs, by their very nature, are "copies" of something else in the sense that they require some other thing to serve as their subject matter. However, a photograph is original in the sense that it is a new and different depiction of its subject matter.

Photographers should also remember that the photograph only, or the negative of it, is considered original; the subject matter or idea embodied in the picture is not.

No one may reproduce your work by making a copy of it without your permission, but anyone may take a photograph of the subject matter depicted in your photograph.

2. Copyright notice

There is no legal requirement in Canada to put a copyright notice on your work. However, it is usually wise to affix the copyright symbol to your work, along with the name of the copyright owner and the year the work was first published.

The copyright symbol is a "c" in a circle, printed as ©. There is no specific place on the work where the notice must appear, but it should be noticeable. Copyright notices on photographs are usually placed at the bottom of the print if there is a border, or on the back if there is no border.

The copyright notice first reminds other people that there is copyright in your work and that you own it. Second, and more important, the notice is necessary to retain copyright protection in countries adhering to the Universal Copyright

Convention. That convention, or treaty, provides that all copies of your work marked with the copyright notice will be given copyright protection in countries that adhere to the convention. Your failure to use the notice on your works may result in the loss of copyright protection in those countries.

3.   Deposit and registration

Registration of copyright, like the notice, is not necessary but very useful. First, registration serves as evidence of the date, owner, and subject matter of copyright. This can be important in a lawsuit. (Note, however, that registration is not conclusive evidence in law because, as discussed below in greater detail, the Registrar of Copyright does not investigate the accuracy of the information filed on applications.)

Second, registration of copyright satisfies people, especially those in countries with more exacting registration and filing requirements, that copyright subsists in a work.

Registering copyright in a work is a simple matter. You need only complete an application form and send it, along with a $35 fee in the form of a certified check or money order made payable to "The Receiver General for Canada," to —

The Registrar of Copyright
Copyright and Industrial Design Branch
50 Victoria Street
Place du Portage, Tower 1
Hull, Quebec
K1A 0C9

(Please note that since fees are subject to change without notice, always check with the Registrar of Copyright first before submitting a fee.)

Registration is effected when the application is accepted. A certificate is then issued to you at no extra cost. See Sample #4 for an example of a completed copyright registration form.

Copies of a work for which registration is sought do not have to be sent to the Registrar of Copyright, nor is there any requirement for verification of the information set out in the application. Because of this latter aspect of registration, the certificate you receive conveys no legal right over and above whatever right you already have in the work; that is, you cannot rely on the certificate to prove a work is original when in fact it isn't.

Note that the owner of copyright is responsible for enforcing it; the Registrar of Copyright does not attempt to prevent others from infringing copyrighted works.

4. Ownership

The ownership of copyright in photographs is a source of frequent dispute between photographers and their clients. The Copyright Act provides that, with two exceptions, the author of the work shall be the first owner of copyright. However, when some other person orders a photographer to take a photograph, and pays him or her as part of that order, then, unless the photographer has an agreement with that person to the contrary, the person who ordered the photograph will own the copyright in it.

Further, if a photographer is employed by someone else to take photographs, the employer owns copyright in the works taken by an employee. However, in this case, if the photographs are taken as part of an article or other contribution to a newspaper, magazine, or other periodical, the employer has copyright to the extent that he or she may publish the photograph in the newspaper, magazine, or periodical, and the photographer has copyright to the extent that he or she can prevent the photograph from being published in some other way.

The greatest difficulty with these provisions of the act arises in situations where the photographer takes a picture of another person without being requested to do so, sells a copy of the photograph and then finds that the person photographed has made copies as well. In such a case, the courts

SAMPLE #4
APPLICATION FOR COPYRIGHT REGISTRATION (CANADA)

Consumer and
Corporate Affairs Canada

Consommation
et Corporations Canada

APPLICATION FOR REGISTRATION OF COPYRIGHT IN A PUBLISHED WORK

FORM 9

(Please print clearly)

I, (we) _____ John Smith _____
(Here insert full name and full address of proprietor(s))

_____ 123 – 1st Street, Anytown, Anyprovince   ZIP 0G0 _____

hereby declare that I am(we are) the owner(s) of the Copyright in the original

_____ Artistic _____ work
(Here insert: literary, dramatic, musical or artistic, as the case may be)

entitled _____ "Rainforest" _____
(Here insert title only (no descriptive matter))

by _____ John Smith _____
(Here insert full name and full address of author(s))

and that the said work was first published by the issue of copies thereof to the public on the

_____ 1st _____ day of _____ January _____ 199-_____
(month)

in the _____ City _____ of _____ Anyprovince _____
(city, town)   (province, state, country)

and I(we) hereby request you to register the Copyright of the said work in my (our) name(s) in accordance

with the provisions of the Copyright Act.

I(We) forward herewith the fee for the examination, registration and issue of a certificate of registration of

copyright.

Dated at _____ Anycity _____ this _____ 15th _____ day of _____ January _____ 199-_____
(city, town)   (month)

John Smith
Signature(s) (See Rule 33)

Copyright and Industrial Design Branch
50 Victoria Street
Place du Portage, Tower I
Hull, Québec
K1A 0C9

| PLEASE DO NOT SEND COPIES OF |
| YOUR WORK TO THE COPYRIGHT OFFICE |

CCA-776 (7 85)

Canada

have held that the photographer owns copyright in the photograph because the person photographed did not order the photograph or make a payment.

5. Duration

The Copyright Act provides that copyright subsists in a photograph for 50 years from the making of the original negative from which the photograph was directly or indirectly derived.

An interesting problem occurs when photographs appear as illustrations in books or magazines. The copyright term for publications is for the life of the author plus 50 years after the author's death. However, the term for photographs is only 50 years from the making of the negative. As a result, it would seem that copyright in a photograph contained in a book may expire long before copyright in the text expires.

A term of copyright cannot be extended; once the 50-year period for a photograph has expired, anyone is free to copy it without penalty.

6. Assignments and licenses

Canadian copyright law permits the owner of copyright to give another person all or part of that right. When the copyright owner sells a right and transfers ownership, it is called an assignment. For example, if a photographer sells to another person the right to reproduce a photograph in the form of posters, without restrictions on the time or place such reproduction could occur, that is considered an assignment.

On the other hand, when a copyright owner sells a right on a temporary basis or for a limited purpose, that is called a license. For example, if a photographer permits a publisher to reproduce a photograph in a book, but in giving such permission specifies that the publisher must do nothing more with the photograph except publish it in the book, the permission is a license.

Most licenses and assignments are set out in document form. The law, however, may sometimes presume an assignment. For example, a court will generally interpret the sale of an article as constituting an assignment of copyright in that article. The courts make this assumption because the law provides that copyright is distinct from the thing that is copyrighted. Thus, it does not follow that a person who buys a photograph automatically acquires copyright in that photograph; the courts presume that the parties have intended that copyright would stay with the photographer. Canadian courts will endeavor to make this presumption, but parties with different intentions can persuade them otherwise.

Assignment and licensing of copyright is dealt with in section 13(4) of the act. That section provides that the owner of copyright may assign his or her right,

> either wholly or partially, and either generally or subject to territorial limitations, and either for the whole term of the copyright or for any other part thereof, and may grant any interest in the right by license,

although an assignment or grant is not valid unless —

(a) it is in writing, and

(b) it is signed by the owner of the right, or his or her authorized agent.

The act does not require a person who receives all or part of copyright by an assignment or license to register the transfer in the copyright office. However, registration is a good idea, because it prevents the original owner of the copyright from transferring the same rights to a second person. If an assignment or license is registered, any subsequent assignments or licenses the original owner attempts to make would be invalid.

You can register an assignment or license by sending evidence (the original and certified copy) of the assignment to the Register of Copyright at the Copyright Office, along with the prescribed fee of $35. (Note that, while fees given are correct at the time of publication, they are subject to change without notice. Always check with the Copyright Office for current fees before submitting any fee.) The copyright office retains the certified copy and returns the original to you with a certificate of its registration.

When drafting a document for assignment or license, it is important to include several items of information. Specifically, the document should set out the full name and address of the person granting the assignment or license, and the full name and address of the person receiving it; the specifics of the grant being given, that is, whether it involves the transfer of ownership, or merely permission for a certain use, and whether there are any limitations on the transfer of ownership or permission for use; the money or other consideration being paid in return for the grant; the date the grant is effective if it is different from the date the document is signed; and at least the signature of the person giving the grant, but preferably the signatures of both parties. The document should also be dated. Two copies should be made — one for each part in the transaction.

A person receiving an assignment or license is entitled to use the work in accordance with the terms of the grant. Such use includes enforcing the right against third parties making a wrongful use of the work. Accordingly, if you grant someone the right to use a photograph in a certain geographical area, and a third party uses the photograph in that area without your permission, you could sue for infringement of copyright. In launching such a suit, you would, of course, be required to prove that you, in fact, owned copyright in the work, which is why it is important to have your assignment or license in writing and registered with the copyright office.

A person who gives an assignment or license is deprived of the right in the work that the assignment or license deals with, unless the grant provides that the transfer of rights is nonexclusive. If the person transferring the right exercises that which has been transferred, the party who has received the right or rights may sue.

For example, in one case, a magazine publisher brought the right to engrave photographs to illustrate a series of articles. After publishing the articles in his magazine, he began distributing them separately, illustrated by engravings from the same photographs. The owner of the copyright in the photographs successfully sued to prevent his publishing the engravings elsewhere, because the publisher's license merely permitted him to engrave the photographs for the magazine.

Even if a person grants all rights in a work, that person may go back to the original source and recreate a work based on that original source. The second work may be identical to the first, but because copyright law only prevent copying, copyright is not infringed. Some courts have effectively limited this principle by implying a condition that a person assigning or licensing copyright will not do anything that renders what he has granted worthless.

You should be careful when selling copyright in a work if you wish to photograph the same subject again. You cannot be certain that the person who bought copyright in the first photograph of the work will not be able to successfully restrain you from taking the same photograph again.

7. Moral rights

The Copyright Act also gives photographers certain other rights in their work, called "moral rights."

Moral rights have nothing to do with morality; the term is a poor translation of a French concept which refers to an author's inherent right to prevent —

(a) the distortion, mutilation or other modification of the author's work,

157

(b) the use of the author's work in association with a product, service, cause or institution,

(c) the author's work being presented to the public anonymously, if the author wishes to be associated with it by name, or, conversely,

(d) the use of the author's name in association with the author's work if he or she wishes to remain anonymous.

The Copyright Act entitles an author to prevent the distortion, mutilation, modification, or association of his or her work only where such an activity prejudices the author's honor or reputation.

Changing the location of a work, or the physical means by which a work is exposed, or the physical structure containing a work (such as a frame) is not by itself a violation of a photographer's moral rights. Moral rights cannot be assigned; they can only be waived.

Assignment of copyright in a work does not by that act alone constitute a waiver of moral rights; there must be some other act, such as signing of an agreement, or the utterance of a statement, or some other act inconsistent with the maintenance of moral rights, for a court to find that moral rights have been waived.

Moral rights endure for the same term as copyright. They may be passed on upon the photographer's death to his or her heirs.

8. Infringement

Infringement occurs when someone copies, sells, rents, distributes, exhibits, or imports a copy of a work without the permission of the copyright owner. Acts of copying that are applicable to photographs include —

(a) production or reproduction of the work or any substantial part of it

(b) converting work into another medium

Copyright is not infringed when someone creates the same work independently by using the same subject matter, or the same concept or idea. For example, it is not copyright infringement of a photograph of the CN Tower in Toronto to go to the same place and take a picture; it would be infringement of copyright only if you took a picture of the original photograph.

Infringement of copyright photographs has been increasing in Canada, despite the easy detection of such infringement. With the popularity of posters and other novelty items, unauthorized copying (or "piracy" as it has become known in the entertainment industry) has become a popular way of making money. In fact, the reproduction of novelty items without permission has become a concern for virtually every major recording or film personality whose work circulates in Canada.

One such case involved the copyright of a photograph of Pope John Paul II. Duomo Inc. obtained copyright in a photograph of the Pope with plans to sell copies in Canada to people wishing to commemorate his visit. Meanwhile, a manufacturer of souvenirs also wished to benefit from the Pope's visit. Without Duomo's permission, the souvenir manufacturer made large quantities of commemorative china bearing the same photograph and proceeded to sell almost $300,000 worth. Duomo sued for copyright infringement and the court ruled in Duomo's favor.

Another case of copyright infringement concerned a different kind of celebrity — a puppet. Universal City Studios sued Zellers Inc. for infringement of copyright in the figure of "E.T., the Extra Terrestrial." In an application to stop Zellers from selling E.T. dolls and credit card key chains, Universal City Studios alleged that its copyright in the artistic work of the sculpture E.T. had been infringed by the defendant's marketing of E.T. dolls without the plaintiff's permission. The court granted Universal's application.

These cases demonstrate how important it is for a photographer to obtain permission from a copyright owner before using someone else's work. Photographers should remember that copyright can exist in almost any literary, scientific, or artistic creation. Paintings, sculptures, drawings, live theater, maps, and engravings are just some of the works covered by copyright.

Parliament has recently emphasized the importance of respecting copyright by increasing the penalties imposed for infringement of copyright. Where a person makes an infringing copy of a work in which copyright subsists or distributes infringing copies for the purpose of trade, he or she could be liable to up to five years' imprisonment or a fine of up to $1 million, or both.

These penalties are in addition to the remedies the Copyright Act gives to the copyright owner. These remedies include the right to collect damages (i.e., monetary compensation), legal costs, an order preventing the reproduction, sale, or distribution of infringing copies and an order requiring the infringer to turn over his or her copies of the work to the copyright owner.

9. Fair use

In certain circumstances a person may reproduce a copyrighted work without permission. Such circumstances are referred to as "lawful use" and are set out in the Copyright Act. The most significant situation of lawful use is "fair use," or as it is referred to in the act, "fair dealing." This section discusses all situations of lawful use referred to in the act that are applicable to photographs and, in particular, those considered by the law to be "fair dealing."

Lawful use can occur in several situations. Those applicable to photographers are as follows:

(a) Where the author of an artistic work, such as a photograph, does not own copyright in that work he or she may use any photographic studies, or earlier versions of a photograph, even though the copyright in the final product belongs to someone else. However, the photographer must not use such material to create the same thing over again.

(b) Certain works that are on public display may be photographed without permission of the copyright owner. The photographs must be of a work of sculpture or artistic craftsmanship that is permanently situated in a public place or building; or it must be an architectural work of art.

Neither "sculpture" nor "work for artistic craftsmanship" are defined in the act. An architectural work of art is defined, however, as

any building or structure having an artistic character or design, in respect of such character or design, or any model for such building or structure.

For example, you could take photographs of the CN Tower, the Parliament Buildings, or a statue in a public place or building, and sell them without permission of the owner of the building or the statue. However, you could not take a photograph of a statue or other work that is on temporary display in a public place or building, or is on display for any length of time in a privately owned building, such as a private gallery or home.

(c) A person may reproduce a work if it is "fair dealing" for the purposes of private study, research, criticism, review, or newspaper summary.

There do not appear to be any cases on this involving photographs, and those cases concerning other types of works are not very helpful.

It would appear, however, from the few cases reported that whether copying would be considered fair depends not only on whether it is for one of the purposes listed in this section, but on

(i)   how much of the work is copied (in other words, whether it is the entire work or just a portion); and

(ii)   whether the original and the copy are likely to compete with each other (in other words, whether people could or would be likely to buy a copy of the work instead of the original). It does not matter whether other people in the same line of work habitually copy without permission, as in the case of newspaper publishers who have been known to copy reports from other publications. Nor does it matter whether the copier acknowledges the source and authorship of the copied work.

The dealing must be "fair," and must be for one of these five purposes and no other. Although there are no cases on photographs to guide you, situations such as the following would probably be covered by this section. For example, this section of the Copyright Act would probably permit a photographer to take a picture of another's copyrighted work without permission, if the picture is made for personal use, such as to study the other person's technique. As well, it would appear that a newspaper might reproduce a few of a photographer's pictures from an exhibit of his work, if the reproduction is for the purpose of reviewing the exhibit, and is not so extensive as to copy the entire show or the best parts of it.

Finally, selections from a book of photographs might lawfully be reproduced without permission if the reproduction is for the purposes of reviewing the book. However, it would not be acceptable in the latter case to reproduce the entire book, even though the reproduction is accompanied by criticism or review; wholesale copying would likely impair the value of the original.

10.   More information

Copies of the Copyright Act and rules may be purchased from any bookstore selling federal government publications, or from

Canadian Government Publishing Centre
Supply and Services Canada
Ottawa, Ontario
K1A 0S9

Any correspondence concerning a copyright application, requests for copies of copyright registration or assignments forms, or inquiries concerning a registration should be directed to

Copyright and Industrial Design Branch
50 Victoria Street
Place du Portage, Tower 1
Hull, Quebec
K1A 0C9

7

THE BUSINESS OF PHOTOGRAPHY

Photographers are often artists first and businesspeople second. They concentrate on the conditions under which their work is produced, instead of the conditions under which it is sold. As a result, photographers do not get fairly paid, they have disputes with clients and suppliers, and they have trouble collecting all their accounts in full.

This chapter reviews ways to reduce these problems and to make the sale of photographic work an easier and more rewarding pursuit.

a.   INSURANCE

The high cost of photographic equipment, the serious financial consequences of a photographer's non-performance, and the risk of damage to property or persons in the course of a shoot make insurance a necessary part of every photographic business.

Insurance is a complex arrangement. The following discussion is designed to simplify its elements and help photographers choose appropriate insurance coverage.

1.   Types of insurance

There are several different types of insurance. Often particular types are governed by standard contracts under state or provincial law. These standard contracts cannot be varied by the insurer or the insured.

The types of insurance most likely to be used by photographers are —

(a) accident and sickness insurance — covers injuries, disabilities, and death,

(b) burglary or theft insurance — covers break and entry, theft by employees, and theft from one's person,

(c) fire insurance, and

(d) liability insurance — covers negligence and accidental loss or damage to goods.

2. Contents of the policy

Most photographers judge insurance by its price. However, this is often the least important aspect; more critical is the scope of the policy.

All policies limit the types of "risks" or perils that are insured against. These limitations can take the form of specific exclusions, such as war, lightning, and flooding. They can also take the form of conditions such as a requirement that there must be evidence that force was used to break and enter a dwelling before a theft will be covered, or that a building not be vacant for longer than a specified number of days in a row.

Before buying insurance, you should identify the risks or perils you want to guard against and then make sure that the policy covers them.

3. Duty of the insured

An insurer's decision to offer insurance and to charge a particular premium is based on an insured's disclosure of information about personal characteristics, business practices, and the type and value of their property. Accordingly, the law obliges the person seeking insurance to disclose all facts known to him or her that might affect the insurer's decision. As one judge put it: "In all cases of insurance, whether on ships, houses, or lives, the underwriter should be informed of every material circumstance within the knowledge of the insured." Put simply, a contract of insurance requires disclosure of every material fact, and someone carrying insurance must act in perfect good faith. If there has been any material untruth, concealment, fraud, or misrepresentation, the insurance policy will be voided and the insurer will be obliged to pay nothing in the event of a loss.

4. Duty of the insurer

Generally speaking, in most cases an insurer is obliged to pay the actual loss suffered by the insured up to the limit of the insurance policy if it occurred while the policy was in force and if the loss occurred as a result of a peril covered by the policy. However, before this obligation arises, the insured must usually prove several things:

(a) A loss occurred

(b) The loss is of a type, or resulted from an event or cause, covered by the policy

(c) The value of the item lost or injury sustained

(d) That the insured had an actual interest in the item lost, or that the injury was actually sustained by him or her, at the time of the loss

(e) The loss occurred while the policy was in force

5. Prompt notice to insurer

Virtually all insurance policies require you to notify the insurer of any loss promptly or, as some policies put it "as soon as practical." This is to enable the insurer to investigate the loss and satisfy itself of the validity and value of the claim.

In most jurisdictions, it is sufficient if the insurer is given sufficient details in a reasonable form; no particular form or medium of notice is usually required.

You will usually also have to complete and file a standard form after having given notice. This form is called a "proof of loss" form and it often must be submitted within a specified time period, sometimes within a few days of the loss.

If you fail to give prompt notice to an insurer or file a proof of loss form, the insurer is usually entitled to deny coverage and pay you nothing.

b. CONTRACTS BETWEEN PHOTOGRAPHERS AND USERS

Contracts between photographers and users are numerous, and they vary according to the type of photographer, the sophistication of the photographer and his or her customer, the intended uses of the work, and the complexity of the job. However, there are some common questions that almost every contract should address.

1. Definition of terms

Does the contract use specialized terms capable of different interpretations or that have no common meaning? For example, does the contract refer to special equipment or techniques? If so, they should be defined in a separate section at the beginning of the contract.

2. Identity of the parties

Whom is the contract between? You should include the proper legal name of the parties, and the following information:

- Whether the client is a partnership, an unincorporated association, a corporation, or a sole proprietorship

- Whether the client is registered and, if so, in what jurisdiction

- Where the client's head office is

- What the legal status of the client is

3. Nature of the work to be performed

In any agreement, make sure that all the details of the work to be done are covered:

- What exactly have you as the photographer been asked to do?

- Where and when is the work to be performed?

- What props or talent are to be used, and who is to choose, supply, and pay for them?

- What is the purpose of the project, and who is to approve or give instructions or make artistic decisions during the project? How are these decisions to be conveyed (e.g., orally, in writing, by letter, or by fax)?

- Does a client representative have to "sign off" or approve certain steps or changes?

- What standard, if any, must be met, and who is to decide whether you have measured up to it? What criteria will be used to measure performance? Does the client have particular requirements concerning format, color, or other matters?

4. Compensation to be paid

Any requirements about fees and expenses must also be in the agreement:

- What fee is the photographer to be paid?

- What expenses are to be paid, and who is to approve them?

- How are expenses to be documented?

- When is the photographer to be paid?

- Must the photographer submit an invoice, and, if so, where should he or she send it, and to whose attention should it be sent?

- How should it be sent? What form should it take?

- If the fee is variable, by what means is it to be calculated?

- What changes in the project will result in a change to the fee or expenses, and who is to make and approve such changes?

- In what form is compensation to be paid? Where is it to be paid? To whom is it to be paid?

- What remedies does the photographer have if he or she is not paid? Is he or she entitled to charge interest and, if so, at what rate?

- Does the client acquire any right to use or gain possession of the photographs if the bill is not paid in full?

5. Cancellation of the project

Provisions should also be in the agreement to protect you in case you cannot complete the work:

- What if the photographer is unable or unwilling to complete his or her tasks under the contract? What is his or her obligation in such circumstances, if any?

- What if the client cancels the project — how is such cancellation to be communicated? What will be the financial consequences of a cancellation? Does the user acquire any right to use or gain possession of material produced before cancellation?

6. Credit

Make sure that the agreement details how any credit to your work is given. Are you to be given any public credit for your work and, if so, how and where is that credit to be given? (This is part of a photographer's moral rights, but is often a specific, separate term.)

7. Copyright and moral rights

Make sure that copyright obligations are clearly defined in the agreement:

- Who is to own copyright in the work produced? What work is your client entitled to use?

- What is the purpose, geographical area, media, and time of such use? Is the right of use limited to the client, or may the client extend that right to some other party? Will you have any prior right of approval of any aspects of use?

- Do you retain your moral rights or are such rights waived? Is the client entitled to distort, modify, or mutilate the work in any way? If so, in what ways? Will you have any prior right of approval?

- If your client breaches the terms of the contract concerning use, will you have the right to prevent such breach by means of an injunction? Will you be entitled to additional compensation and, if so, how will it be calculated?

8. Rights to future use of work

The agreement must set out your future rights to the work, if any:

- If the client wishes to extend or expand its use in any way, will he or she be able to do so? How and to whom will the client communicate his or her intention?

- Will you be paid more for such additional use, and, if so, how is that additional compensation to be calculated? Is the client's extension or expansion of use subject to your prior right of approval?

9. Delivery and loss of material

Make sure that the agreement sets out who is responsible for delivery of the finished work:

- Who is responsible for getting the finished photographic material to the client, the client's printer, or other supplier — the client, the printer or other supplier, or you?

- If your work is lost, stolen, or damaged after it leaves your premises, who is to be responsible?

- Who pays for shipping? Who pays in the event of loss, theft, or damage? How is such payment to be calculated — a set fee per transparency, for example, or the cost of a reshoot? Is any party obliged to obtain and pay for insurance to compensate for such loss, theft, or damage?

- Is the client, printer or other supplier, or you, the photographer, obliged to give the other parties notice of loss, theft, or damage, or will it be presumed after the expiration of a prescribed period? If notice is to be given, how is it to be given, to whom, and within what time period? If notice is not given in compliance with these rules, what happens?

10.   Miscellaneous

Make sure that the agreement states which jurisdiction shall apply:

- If the client and photographer are located in different jurisdictions, or if the work is to be performed in a jurisdiction other than the one in which the client and photographer reside, whose law is to govern the parties' relationship?

- How is the contract to be amended — in writing? orally? either of these?

- Does the written contract contain the entire bargain, or are there other discussions or documents that contain terms that affect the parties' relationship?

- Is timely performance and payment an important term?

171

- If one or more terms of the contract is found to be unenforceable or ineffective at law, can it be severed from the rest of the agreement, or does the whole contract fail?

11. Execution of the contract

The agreement must set out how each party is to signify his or her approval:

- How are each of the parties to indicate their approval and acceptance of the contract? (A signature is most common.) If a person is signing on behalf of a corporation, what position does he or she hold? Does he or she have authority to bind the corporation? (If so, this should be specifically stated.)

- If the person is signing as an individual, is he or she the age of majority, competent, and acting freely? If you have any doubt about a person's age, consider having a guardian sign on his or her behalf. If you have doubt about his or her mental competency, have him or her obtain independent legal advice, and obtain confirmation from his or her legal counsel that such advice has been given.

- Consider having someone witness each signature on the contract.

c. CONTRACTS BETWEEN PHOTOGRAPHERS AND STOCK PHOTOGRAPHY AGENCIES

Stock photography agencies are an increasingly important bridge between photographers and consumers. A stock photo agency usually acquires some interest in a photographer's work; it may obtain a long-term license or a complete assignment of the copyright. Occasionally, however, it may act merely as an agent for the photographer. The stock photo agency then promotes the photographer's work to potential clients, typically by means of an annual catalog displaying samples from its collection.

The agency typically sends sample transparencies to potential customers. If a customer likes what he or she sees, the stock photo agency will sell the customer a temporary license, monitor the customer's actual use, collect a fee from such use, and remit a portion of that fee back to the photographer.

Stock photo agencies also often take legal action on behalf of photographers to prevent customers from exceeding their license.

Stock photo agencies benefit both photographers and customers. They allow customers to have access to a huge body of photographic work at a fraction of the cost it would require to produce the work from scratch, and they allow photographers to contact, negotiate with, and collect from, a huge pool of potential customers more cheaply than the photographer could do on his or her own.

Because stock photo agencies are so important to photographers and their customers, it's important for an agency to consider these questions before entering into an agreement with a photographer.

- Is the photography original?

- Is the photographer the author of the work and the owner of copyright in it?

- Are there "similars" or duplicates of the photography in existence, and, if so, what prohibition will be imposed on their use or sale by the photographer?

- How is the agency's compensation to be calculated? What expenses is it entitled to deduct from gross amounts it receives?

- How often must it pay the photographer and render a statement? What form should that statement take?

Who is responsible for bad debts, taxes, collection expenses, and other costs?

- In what markets is the agency entitled to market the photographer's work? Is this arrangement exclusive?

- Is the photographer entitled to conduct assignment photography on his or her own?

- Is the agency entitled to sell the photographer's work for whatever price and conditions it wishes, or are there certain minimums in the case of a buy-out, for example?

- Is the photographer obliged to obtain model releases, and, if so, in what form are they to be? Does the agency have its own form, for example?

- How is the photographer to submit his or her work?

- Is the agency to ensure the photographer always receives credit when his or her work is used, and, if so, what form should that credit take?

- What specifically is the agency to do about storage, care, and marketing of photographs? What happens if photographic work is lost or damaged while in the care or control of the agency or one of the agency's clients?

- How long is the license arrangement between the agency and the photographer to run? May it be terminated early and, if so, on what grounds?

- If the agreement is terminated, what happens to the photographic work possessed by the agency and to licenses given by it?

- Is the agency entitled or obliged to enforce the photographer's copyright? If so, how are legal expenses to be handled? What obligations does the photographer have if there is a lawsuit? Who is responsible for hiring a lawyer?

- What happens if the agency is sold or goes bankrupt?

d. CONTRACTS BETWEEN STOCK PHOTO AGENCIES AND USERS

Stock photo agencies must also define any obligations to their clients. They must state what rights in the photographic work the use is purchasing — an assignment of copyright, or a license? If a license is being granted, how is it limited? For example, is it limited by time, geographic area, medium, number of reproductions, or purpose? Is the license transferable?

Here are some other questions that should be considered in any contract between a stock photo agency and a user:

- When is the user entitled to exercise its license — upon receipt of the negatives, or upon the agency's receipt of payment in full?

- What if the agency is not paid — what remedies is it to have against the user?

- What if the user loses or damages the photographic work? Who pays, and how much?

- What if the user exceeds his or her license by using the photographic work too long or too many times? What remedies does the agency have? What fee, if any, is to be paid and how is it to be calculated?

- Is the user entitled to make and retain copies of the photographic work, or must it return all copies upon the expiration of its license?

- Is the agency to have any control of the use, such as a prior right of approval if copy or editorial is to be used in conjunction with the photographic work?

- Is any credit to be given to the photographer? If so, what form should it take?

175

- How is a request for license to be made, and how is its acceptance to be indicated? Who has authority to grant such a license?

- Is the agency to provide a model release if any talent appears in the photograph chosen by the user?

- How is use to be verified? Are tear sheets to be sent, or is the agency entitled to audit the user's books and records?

e. CONTRACTS BETWEEN STOCK PHOTO AGENCIES AND ADVERTISING AGENCIES

One of the biggest markets for photography is advertising. For photographers, advertising is one of the biggest areas of difficulty.

The most common areas of dispute between photographers and advertisers or their agencies are unmet deadlines, failure to produce satisfactory work, inadequate communication and planning, what photographic rights are being bought and sold, and late payments.

A contract that addresses the questions set out earlier in this chapter under section **c.** will help the parties cope with almost all of these and other problems. Photographers would be well advised to specifically raise these potential problems and pose solutions to them before taking on work. The resulting contract may not be completely favorable, but at least it will be clear.

If the project is large or has a great element of risk, a lawyer should be hired to help draft the contract.

f. GETTING PAID

A photographer can spend substantial amounts of money in the course of a shoot, on film, chemicals, props, talent, site fees, transportation, insurance, etc. Because a photographer's up-front expenses can be high, it is particularly important that he or she get paid fully and promptly.

Collecting accounts is never easy. Keen competition among photographers and economic uncertainty among clients make collection a perennial problem. Photographers are made to feel that if they insist on either prompt payment or a fair price, the client will go elsewhere. The problem is further exacerbated by bad business habits both on the part of photographers and their clients. These include informal recordkeeping, infrequent documentation, and tardy billing.

Set out below are a few suggestions which should help reduce disputes between photographers and their clients and improve collection of photographers' accounts.

1. Investigate your client's credit worthiness

The best way of avoiding bad debts is to avoid doing business with people who are unable to pay you. Before assuming any large prospect, a photographer should ask to see if the potential client is credit worthy. Better Business Bureaus, trade publications, trade associations, and court records (particularly those that keep records of security interests and other charges against property) are all important sources of information.

Find out if the potential client has lawsuits pending against it, if it is in a troubled industry, or if it has it a good reputation with its customers in its industry.

2. Have a written contract

If you have to sue to collect your fee, you must prove that the client instructed you to undertake the job and that he or she agreed to pay for the work. A written contract is the best evidence of such an arrangement. An oral (i.e., verbal) agreement may still be effective and enforceable, but it is a lot harder to prove.

3. Keep a written record

Always keep a written record of problems that arise in the course of a project:

- Were there changes in the project, either at the client's request or because of external circumstances?

- What work was performed?

- What expenses were incurred?

Even a handwritten note will do; it may serve as evidence, or at least as an aid to your memory if a lawsuit arises at some later date. Almost all professionals do this. Lawyers often call such notes "memos to file"; advertising and public relations practitioners often call them "call reports," "activity sheets," or "dockets."

It is also helpful to send your client copies of such records when they are made. If the client disputes the content of the record, it is reasonable to assume that he or she will make it known promptly. This way, disputes can be identified at an early point in the process. Moreover, if the client does not dispute the content of your record, it can create a presumption that your records are accurate and fairly reflect the activity they purport to describe.

4. Obtain some money in advance

Photographers should consider obtaining deposits in advance of performing work. These deposits could cover disbursements or reflect some mutually acceptable percentage of the total bill. The photographer's contract should characterize this money as a "deposit." The law has long held that in most cases the deposit is forfeited or given up by the client if he or she cancels the agreement after entering into it.

Photographers should also consider requesting progress payments so that the client pays the total fee in installments while the work is being performed. Progress payments are especially useful when a job is performed over a long period of time.

Finally photographers should consider exchanging proofs, negatives, or positives only when some or all of the agreed fee has been paid. Alternatively, photographers should specify in their contract that —

(a) both property and copyright in all work they produce remains vested in the photographer until and unless the photographer is paid in full; and

(b) the client acquires no right, title, or interest in, or right to use, the photographs until and unless the photographer is paid in full.

5. Render accounts promptly

Clients are more willing to pay if the memory of your hard work, good service, and professional product is still fresh in their minds. Follow your accounts up with regular reminder letters if payment is not promptly received. Keep copies of these letters and proof of postage or delivery for use in court if that should become necessary.

6. Pursue delinquent accounts

If a client has not paid within a set period such as 60 or 90 days, collection action should be taken immediately. The client may fall into financial difficulty, or may forget your project, if you do not move quickly. Moreover, a client is likely to be less appreciative of your work, and therefore less willing to pay your bill, if your work is not fresh in his or her mind. Your bill will be viewed less favorably if the client can barely remember the services for which he or she is being billed.

Prompt collection efforts also tell the client you are serious and persistent; this, too, increases the chances of getting paid because the client will realize you won't go away just because you have been ignored.

GLOSSARY

APPROPRIATION OF PERSONALITY

The use of a person's voice, mannerisms, or appearance for commercial purposes without permission.

ASSIGNMENT

A transaction that transfers the entire benefit of a contract to a third party (such as a contract giving rights to reproduce a photograph). The person giving away the benefit, or the ownership, is called the *assignor*, and the person receiving it is the *assignee*.

COMMERCIAL USE

Use for profit or other benefit, such as publicity. Commercial use in the context of photograph includes sale, advertising, rental, entry in photographic competitions where there is a monetary award, use in art produced for sale, and possibly display in a store.

COMMON LAW

The body of law that has arisen as a result of decisions made by judges in areas not covered by statute law — that is, the law that has grown out of principles and customs, rather than from government.

CONSIDERATION

Something of value in the eyes of the law that is given for a promise in order to make the contract enforceable. Consideration may be a sum of money, a promise to do something, or the delivery of some property.

CONTRACT

An agreement giving rise to obligations that are enforced or recognized by law.

COPYRIGHT

The right to produce or reproduce a work or any substantial part of the work. (See chapter 6 for details.)

CURRENCY

The bank notes, paper money, or bank or government securities of a country.

DAMAGES

The monetary compensation awarded by a court to a plaintiff in a lawsuit. Damages are paid by the defendant.

DEFAMATION

A statement that degrades an individual in the eyes of his or her fellow citizens and exposes him or her to hatred, contempt, or ridicule. To be considered defamatory a statement must be false.

DEFENDANT

A party in a civil lawsuit whom another party alleges has done some wrongful act and caused that other party damage.

FAIR USE

The legal use of a copyrighted work without the copyright owner's permission. Fair use includes use for purposes of criticism, comment, news, reporting, scholarship, and research.

HARASSMENT

Conduct that is unreasonably annoying and persistent. It could include following a person from place to place, continually watching his or her house, threatening or intimidating him or her, or blocking or obstructing his or her path. A person who harasses another may be subject to criminal charges and a civil prosecution.

INFRINGEMENT

Use of a copyright work without the copyright owner's permission and which is not fair use.

LIBEL

A defamatory statement expressed in permanent form, such as in writing. It is contrasted with slander, which is a defamatory statement that is spoken.

LICENSE

The limited transfer of an interest or right in something, where the party receiving the license does not permanently acquire full rights on the subject matter.

NUISANCE

Conduct that unreasonably interferes with someone's personal freedom, discomposes or injuriously affects the senses or the nerves, or is an affront to the dignity and is done without justification.

OFFICIAL SECRETS

Information designated under the Official Secrets Act in Canada, and under sections 795 and 796 of Title 18 of the United States Code in the United States. Official secrets typically include information pertaining to military installations and equipment, battle plans, defense strategies, and weaponry.

PERMISSION

Formal consent, preferably in writing, and signed by both parties.

PERSONALITY

Qualities that are capable of imitation or appropriation, such as a person's voice, mannerisms, or appearance.

PLAINTIFF

A party who initiates a lawsuit.

PRIVACY

Defined differently in different jurisdictions. It is sometimes used to mean the right to be left alone, and other times it means one's personality.

PUBLIC PLACE

A place in which the public is free to enter without restriction or charge, and which is not owned by a private party. Public places generally include streets and sidewalks, public parks, and government buildings to which the public is normally admitted.

RELEASE

A contract containing the consent of a person to have his or her picture used by another. It sets out the types of use that may be made of the photograph, the person who is permitted to make such use, and the payment, if any, that is made in return for the release being given.

RIGHT TO PRIVACY

Depending on the jurisdiction, the right to be left alone or, alternatively, the right to contract the manner and extent of the use of one's personality for commercial purposes.

SEAL

A paper wafer attached to a contractual document. Traditionally, a seal signifies a document of great importance and symbolizes the parties' recognition of the significance and formality of their agreement. Consequently, if a contract bears a seal, consideration is not normally required for the contract to be enforceable.